A Prisoner in

John Still

Alpha Editions

This edition published in 2024

ISBN 9789362515735

Design and Setting By
Alpha Editions
www.alphaedis.com
Email - info@alphaedis.com

Contents

FOREWORD

THIS book, like most books, consists both of facts and opinions. In order to fortify the facts, and so that it may be clearly seen that the opinions are justified, a number of extracts from the "Report on the Treatment of British Prisoners of War in Turkey," which was presented to Parliament in November, 1918, are included here by the special permission of the Controller of His Majesty's Stationery Office. So few people read Government publications that this course seems necessary.

In this official report it is stated that out of 16,583 British and Indian prisoners "Believed Captured," 3,290 are dead, and 2,222 untraced and almost certainly dead. But this report was compiled before the end of the war and is admittedly incomplete. I do not know the actual statistics, viii which must by now be available, nor do I know where to obtain them. But, as stated in the book, we in Turkey believed that about 75 per cent. of the British rank and file perished within two years of being captured. It may be that we were unduly pessimistic; it is very sincerely to be hoped that we were, and on the whole it seems probable. But I leave the figure unaltered in the text, for it was our sincere belief after very difficult and laborious enquiries made secretly. In the official report the figures show that of a total of 4,932 British believed captured, no less than 2,289 are either dead or untraced. This amounts to 46 per cent. It would be interesting to know the final figures.

The extracts taken from the report have been selected because they are either general in character or have special reference to Angora or Afion Kara Hissar, the two camps I knew personally.

I am indebted to three fellow-prisoners for the photograph reproduced as a frontispiece to this book, for the piece of music, for reading the MS., and for reading the proofs.

EXTRACTS FROM A REPORT ON THE TREATMENT OF BRITISH PRISONERS OF WAR IN TURKEY.

The history of the British prisoners of war in Turkey has faithfully reflected the peculiarities of the Turkish character. Some of these, at any rate to the distant spectator, are sufficiently picturesque; others are due to the mere dead-weight of Asiatic indifference and inertia; others again are actively and resolutely barbarous. It has thus happened that at the same moment there have been prisoners treated with almost theatrical politeness and consideration, prisoners left to starve and die through simple neglect and incompetence, and prisoners driven and tormented like beasts. These violent inconsistencies make it very difficult to give a coherent and general account of the experience of our men. Almost any unqualified statement can be contradicted again and again by undoubted facts; and the whole subject seems often to be ruled by nothing but pure chance.

Yet on the whole there are two principles which may be detected as influencing the behaviour of the Turk in this matter, first and last, one being an affair of deliberate policy, the other instinctive and customary. Mixed in with a good deal of easy-going kindness, there is always to be found the conviction that it can matter little what becomes of the ordinary mass, so long as compliments are paid to the great. It has doubtless been a real surprise to the Turkish mind, even in high places, to learn that the rights of the common soldier are seriously regarded by western opinion— the rights, moreover, of a few thousand disarmed men who could be no longer used in battle. This principle has not always been effective, it must be added, in its application to prisoners of higher rank, as some of the following pages will abundantly show; but it has seldom failed in the treatment of the rank and file. These have had small reason in their helplessness to regard the Turk as that chivalrous and honourable foe of whom we have sometimes heard.

It need scarcely be said that the level of surgical and medical skill is low in Turkey. There are good doctors, but not many of them, and it is only in Constantinople that they are to be found. In the provincial towns the hospitals are nearly always places of neglect and squalor, where a sick man is simply left to take his chance of recovery, a chance greatly compromised by Turkey's total indifference to the first rudiments of sanitation. Such hospitals are naturally the last to be provided with adequate stock or equipment of any kind; and even if some modern appliance is by fortune forthcoming, it will probably be beyond the local talent to make use of it. In a very horrible Red Crescent hospital at Angora, for example, there was at one time seen an excellent German disinfecting apparatus standing idle amidst the filth, because no one could tell how it was worked. It is fair to say that in such places there is no distinction between the treatment of prisoners and that of Turkish sick or wounded; all suffer alike by reason of a state of civilisation centuries out of date.

It was characteristic, too, that until the end of 1916, or even later, the only clearing-station that existed in the city, where the men discharged from hospital were collected until they could be sent into the interior, was apparently the common civil prison, a most vile and filthy place, in which many of our men lay for weeks until the convenient moment happened to come for removing them. At first they were lodged there in ordinary cells; later they would occupy the gallery of a large hall, where their tedium was relieved by witnessing the vociferous floggings of xii the criminals on the floor below. This would seem to be the same prison as that in which certain British naval officers have at different times undergone most barbarous punishment (in the name of "reprisals"), by being confined for many weeks underground, without sight of day, in solitude and severe privation. As a collecting place for prisoners from hospital it was superseded in 1917 by a camp at Psamatia, a suburb of the city, installed in a disused Armenian school and church. This was at first a dirty and disagreeable place; though supposed to be in some measure for convalescents, it was always a struggle to get so much as a wash there; but under a better commandant it was improved later on.

But before going further we may give what is in effect the substance of our whole report—the epitome, in unmistakable terms, of the story of the prisoners' treatment. The officially announced figures of the mortality among them, so far as are known up to the present date, give the exact measure of the meaning of captivity in Turkey. The total number of officers and men believed to have been taken prisoners by the Turks from the beginning of the war is 16,583. Of these 3,290 have been reported dead, while xiii 2,222 remain untraced, and we must believe that they, too, have almost all perished unnamed, how or where we cannot tell in any single case. They all belonged to the force which surrendered at Kut, and it is therefore certain that they passed living into Turkish hands, but not one word was ever afterwards heard of any of them. The story we shall now tell is the only light that can now be thrown upon their fate.[1]

Afion, indeed, has a hideous record for the flogging of prisoners—punishment which was habitual there, for the most trifling offences, while the place was under the control of a certain Turkish naval officer. This man ruled with a cow-hide whip, from which the offender received a given number of lashes on his bare back. Many specific instances are known and noted. Fortunately the man's behaviour became notorious, and the Turkish

Government, under pressure, removed him early in 1917. He had had time, however, to add to the burden of the unhappy men from Kut, whose appearance when they reached Afion is vividly remembered by the prisoners who were already there. Some of them naked, many half out of their minds with exhaustion, most of them rotten with dysentery, this band of survivors was received with deep sympathy by the rest, who did all they might to restore them, small as their own resources were. In very many cases it was too late. The sick men were placed in the camp hospital; but this was a hospital in not much more than the name, for though there was a Turkish doctor in attendance, with some rough Turkish orderlies, medicines were non-existent, and a man too ill to look after himself had a very poor chance. Deaths were frequent; the dead were buried by their comrades in the Christian cemetery of the town. All this time, close at hand, there was a party of British officers imprisoned at Afion, xv two of whom were officers of the medical service. Yet all communication between officers and men was flatly forbidden, under heavy penalty, throughout the bad time of 1916 and even later. English doctors had thus to wait inactive, knowing that the men were dying almost daily, a few yards off, for mere want of proper care.

Angora is another camp which began very badly. In the spring of 1917 (it had already been in use for a year and a half) there were seventy-five prisoners lodged here in two rooms of a very insanitary house, which caused outbreaks of typhus. There was a brutal sergeant-major in charge and a free use of the whip. Conditions have improved as Angora has become the centre of the working groups engaged in laying the narrow-gauge line towards Yozgad. By May, 1917, the chief settlement was under canvas, in a healthy position about twenty miles from the town, moving forward as the work progressed. A little later we hear of kind treatment on the part of the Turkish officers. By the end of the year there was rather a large concentration of British prisoners in this district; and although they were short of clothing and suffered much xvi from the winter cold—snow was thick in December—the general treatment was considerate. The men appear to have considerably impressed the Turks by their power of bearing up and adapting themselves to hard circumstances.

The Turkish Government has announced that in its zeal for the comfort of the British officers in its hands, the finest situations in Asia Minor have been chosen for their internment; and if a prisoner of war were in the position of a summer tourist in peace-time this consideration would be admirable. Yozgad, Kastamuni, Afion-Kara-Hissar, Gedis, are places of interest and beauty; the mountain scenery of Central Anatolia is very striking, the summer climate excellent. Unfortunately this attractive landscape is buried deep in snow throughout the winter; the cold is intense, the places named being from three to four thousand feet above sea-level; communication with the outer world (Afion alone is on the railway) becomes difficult or almost impossible; and the picturesque towns, with their streams and valleys and mediæval citadels, have none but the most primitive provision against the rigour of the season. This would be so even in the time of peace. The difficulties of life under such conditions xvii in war-time can hardly be imagined—difficulties partly due to the general scarcity of necessities, but also much aggravated by Turkish incompetence and disorganisation. With each winter the officers have had to face the prospect of something like famine and destitution, well knowing that they must rely on their own hampered efforts, if they were to get through.

In writing of them one must, in fact, put aside all idea that the care of prisoners is the business of their captors. In Turkey it has amounted to this—that British officers have been sent to live in places where at least it is very hard to keep body and soul together—have there been put under various restrictions and disadvantages—and have then been left to support themselves as best they might. They have had to pay for practically everything they needed beyond bare housing, and sometimes even for this.

After Broussa the most conveniently placed camp, so far as officers are concerned, is Afion-Kara-Hissar, though its direct communication with the capital by railway did not save the prisoners from severe privation in the winter of 1917-18. The few things there were to buy were then at prohibitive cost; and the general state of affairs may be judged by the fact that on Christmas Day, there being no firewood and twenty degrees of frost, the officers took their dinner in bed, as the only place where they could keep a little warm. Afion was one of the earliest formed prison camps in Turkey. In the spring of 1918 there were 100 British officers here, and 120 Russians. This is too large a number for the accommodation, and still more for the resources of the town.

They are lodged in a number of empty houses between the town and the station, which is about two miles away. These houses are in two groups, forming the so-called upper and lower camps, though they are not camps in the sense of being enclosed in any sort of compound. They seem to be fairly satisfactory in good weather, but they are very primitive. In the buildings, more or less unfinished, of the lower camp there was at first no provision for heating and no glass in the windows. By the early part of 1917 the officers had arranged a routine for themselves which the vexatious, sometimes maddening, inefficiency and caprice of the Turk did not seriously interfere with. They had books and games indoors, fixed hours of study, and a flourishing run of amateur theatricals. Out of doors they were cramped, but there were some xix limited chances of cricket. Once a week the two camps could visit each other, under escort, and there was another weekly outing when they could go for country walks.

The constant trial was not bad treatment, but the stupid and irritating notions of the commandant and his subordinates on the score of discipline. The natural indolence, the want of organisation, the dirty habits and customs of the Turks, their inveterate and irrational lying, all meant a wearisome wastage of time and temper. The commandant had the mark of the typically incompetent manager—a fondness for imposing sudden and teasing regulations, without the will to enforce them consistently. Thus at one time it was decreed that everyone must be fully dressed for the 8 a.m. roll-call, at another that all lights must be out by 9.30 in the evening, at another that no officer should rest on his bed during the day; such rules would be rigidly insisted upon for a few days, till the novelty wore off, and then helplessly abandoned. It is recorded, indeed, that soon after the "lights out" rule was started, the commandant himself dropped in at 11 p.m. one night to visit the officers of the lower camp; he found them all up, stayed for a talk and a glass of Greek brandy, and made no further allusion to the matter. This is the amiable side of the Turkish misrule. It is the other that has since become prominent at Afion, till the place compared badly with other camps for the stupid tyranny of its control. It is not surprising if the officers have felt themselves back in an ill-managed nursery, with its rotation of indulgence and random severity.

Here for the present ceases our information with regard to the officers' camps in Asia Minor. There are others—Eskichehir and Konia—which are reserved for Indian officers only; but of these little is known beyond the fact that the prisoners enjoy complete local freedom. Eskichehir was supposed to be the "depôt modèle" of the empire, and the late Sultan even ordained that the officers there might keep their swords. But so far as the British officers are concerned, our sketch will have indicated the main lines of their daily routine, its security on the whole from the worst forms of coercion, and on the other hand its exposure to grave risk and hardship. Fully to understand what their existence is like, one must of course amplify the picture in many ways, the chief of which is perhaps the deadly monotony of its isolation. All communication with the world outside is endlessly uncertain and broken. Between xxi these prisoners and their friends at home, who only ask to be allowed to send them the help they need, there lies a mass of corrupt and torpid inefficiency, a barrier almost impossible to overcome because incalculable and irrational. The due and punctual censoring of the prisoners' mails, for example, has apparently been beyond the resources of the Turkish Empire. The authorities have never been able to establish any system by which parcels, letters and books, might be regularly scrutinised at the various camps. These are all dealt with at Constantinople, with long and exasperating delays. A novel for an hour's reading, say, is delivered to an officer in Asia Minor; it will instantly be taken from him, returned to the Capital, and there lost to sight for months before it is discovered to be inoffensive and allowed to proceed. For a long while the prisoners' letters were cut down to the barest minimum both in number and length, because the censor at headquarters could not deal with more. It appears that it has not been possible to carry out this work in the camps for the highly Turkish reason that the various authorities concerned mistrusted each other too deeply.

The housing, feeding, and medical care of the prisoners, the delivery of their parcels and correspondence, their pay, the exchange of invalids and others, the inspection of internment camps, and the thousand and one details of the treatment of prisoners, have been the subject of constant attention and voluminous correspondence, hampered not only by the callous obstinacy of the Turkish Government, but by the failure of Turkish officials even to read the communications addressed to them.

CHAPTER I

THE DARDANELLES

AT dawn on the 9th of August, 1915, the 6th Battalion of the East Yorkshire Regiment received an order to attack the great hill that towers above Anafarta. The order was late, hours too late, for the messenger had lost his way; so, although we did not know it at the time, we had already forfeited our chance, and were launched upon a forlorn endeavour.

The rampart of hills to the east of us was black against the chill, pale sky as we moved out across the grey flats that led up to the foot of Teke Tepe, towering up to nearly 1,000 feet ahead of us. And we came under fire from our right flank almost from the very start.

The foot-hills of the range were rough with boulders, and deep cut by rocky ravines. As we moved on and on, up and up, men got lost in the prickly scrub oak, holly they called it, and it became increasingly difficult to maintain any sort of formation. But the enemy's fire grew in volume as we mounted, poured into us at ever decreasing range from the right and from the front.

In that hour my admiration for the splendid courage of the men rose to a pitch of exaltation. They were Yorkshire miners for the most part, dogged, hard men of the sturdiest breed on earth. Those who were hit stayed where they fell, and those who were whole climbed on. The only complaint heard upon that hill-side was that no enemy could be seen to fire upon. So there was but little reply from our rifles as we went on up.

About thirty of us reached the top of the hill, perhaps a few more. And when there were about twenty left we turned and went down again. We had reached the highest point and the furthest point that British forces from Suvla Bay were destined to reach. But we naturally knew nothing of that. All that we knew was that the winding ravine down which we retreated alternately exposed us to rifle fire from the enemy above and protected us. Hid us and revealed us. A sapper major who walked with me, after a long silence said, "Are you married?" "Yes," I replied. "It it were not for that this would be good fun," said the major. So we agreed that if one of us got out he should go and see the other's wife. And it fell to me to do it; for he was shot through the ankle soon after that, and an hour later was bayoneted in cold blood by a Turk.

We hoped that the foot of the ravine would bring us out among our own supports at the bottom of the hill. But the enemy held it.

Five out of all those who had gone up got down again alive.

We reached the point where the ravine ended, and in the scrub ahead of us we saw a number of men who fired upon us. For a moment we thought they were our own, firing in ignorance. Then we saw that they were Turks. We had run into the back of an enemy battalion which held the lower slopes against our supports. They had crossed the range at a point lower than that we had attacked, and had cut in behind our climbing force. We could do nothing but surrender.

When we held up our hands some dozen or more of the enemy charged towards us with fixed bayonets. And we began to experience that strange mixture of nature, so characteristic of the Turks, from which we and our fellows were to suffer much in the years to come.

The man who took possession of me searched my pockets and annexed everything of military use except my revolver, which had fallen out of my hand a minute before, when I had been knocked down by a bullet that glanced off a rock on to my leg. He took out my purse and saw that it contained five sovereigns in gold (more than I have ever seen since) and a good deal in silver. Then he gave it back to me, and apparently told me to keep it. The pay of a Turkish private is, or was, ten piastres *a month*, nominally about one shilling and eightpence. My captor was a good Turk. Later on, when I came to know how rare good Turks were, I was filled with marvel.

Of those taken with me, one was not molested; one was fired at from five yards' distance, missed, and quietly captured; one was beaten and fired at. Thank God the man who fired at him hit the man who was beating him and broke his wrist. The fourth, my Colonel, was bayoneted. Then, for the moment their fury ceased. I was permitted to tend the Colonel. He did not seem to suffer pain at all, only to be intensely thirsty. He drank the whole of the contents of my water-bottle as well as his own. They even allowed me to carry him on my back; and on my back the Colonel died. May he rest in peace! He was a brave man, and a good friend to me.

Brief though my personal experience of battle was, it has left two lasting convictions. One that wounds from which men die are rarely painful, at any rate for a considerable time after they have been inflicted. And another that men actually in action neither fear nor even expect death. As we climbed up that hill on August the 9th; as we dwindled down to fifty, to thirty, to twenty; as we retreated down that winding, trench-like ravine, and dwindled to five, I was not blind. I was not even fighting, but only being fought. There was but little chance to fire back, and only once did I get a bead on an enemy target. There was nothing extraordinarily exciting about it. Mostly it was hard work, rough and prickly, and I was tired. My brain was quite clear. I saw and realized the odds. But I never expected to be killed, though I knew for certain that nearly everyone else would be. It was not courage, for I have trembled with fear on other occasions. It is my fixed belief that this is the ordinary and instinctive attitude of the normal mind. And it is very comforting.

For a time that ranks in my memory longer than some years, and which may have endured for an hour, we were held prisoners just behind the Turkish fighting line. We had been joined by one other captured private and were again five. It was not a pleasant time. Several times we were apparently condemned to death. Once an officer took out his pistol to shoot us and was prevented by a priest, an Imâm with a turban on, who wrestled with him and took his pistol away. Once Derrick and I, the two officers, were put up against a bank to be bayoneted: an unpleasant, ticklish sensation as the steel swings back. But somehow or other it did not come off. When the Turks pushed we were fairly safe; and when our friends pushed the guards threatened to kill us. Personally, I confess to very torn emotions regarding that small section of that particular battle, though it may seem cowardly to do so. I did not honestly hope the Turks would be pushed back just then.

My slight wound was tied up, and we received at last an order to move to the rear. An order from an Asiatic when you have lived for eighteen years in Asia is a strange experience. I disliked it.

Two guards with loaded rifles and fixed bayonets took us back over the hill once more. We wound wearily and painfully up a ravine more or less parallel to the one we had come down. All the way we were meeting enemy reinforcements hurrying to the fighting-line, most of them carrying cardboard boxes of cartridges. Rough, brigand-like fellows they seemed, but very fine infantry. They were the pick of the Ottoman army. Twice our guards had to stand before us and beat off would-be assassins with the butts of their rifles, and once I was struck heavily across the head by a sword-bayonet, but saved by my topee. The whole thing seemed then and still seems rather like a dream, and we walked as men detached from our surroundings.

Near the top of the hill the ravine grew steeper, and at last ended. An aeroplane, one of our own, was circling round the summit of Teke Tepe, spotting for the naval guns; and we all lay low while British shells burst on the rocks about us. The only Turks they seemed likely to harm were our guards. For, far below we could see that a battle was in progress. We could see the white crusted salt on the lake, and the pinkish-brown of Lala Baba hill, from which I had watched, three days before, the storming of Chocolate Hill, like a scene in a theatre. There were British transports in the bay, and outside were British warships cruising slowly while puffs of smoke broke from their sides. These were the last British ships we were to see for more than three years.

We had to run over the crest of the hill, and down a little way into safety on the other side, safety from our own guns. And for the first time I think we felt the pang of lost children. Out of sight of our ships seemed somehow much further than did the other side of the hill from all touch with England.

We halted in safety and sat down, out of breath, while our guards fraternized with a small party of Turkish soldiers and smoked cigarettes. Then we moved on again, and passed away into Turkey.

Worn and very, very thirsty, we were taken that afternoon to the headquarters of General Liman von Sanders, Commander-in-Chief of the enemy forces on Gallipoli; and there we found some more of our men with one more officer. Von Sanders was looking at the samples he had drawn. He has been accused of many things since then, for all I know quite justly; but to us he was not unkind. His staff gave us a meal in their quarters, and he gave two Turkish pounds to our men. But the kindness to the men did not extend far beyond his sight. When next we saw them, some ten days later, they described how their Turkish guards had robbed them of their boots and made them run for several miles barefoot over rough ground. Still, to us the General was civil, though he did say that International Law no longer existed. One of his staff, a German naval officer, told us that they found it almost impossible to get the Turks to take prisoners, or, having taken them, to keep them alive. We, too, had observed this reluctance.

From Liman von Sanders's headquarters to the Turkish general headquarters was about three miles by the way we went, and we arrived there after dark. We were four officers now, all of the 11th Division, and we did not see our men again until much later, in Constantinople.

We were kept in a tent for three days at the Turkish G.H.Q., and were not troubled with many questions. Our interrogation came later. Various officers came to see us. To look at us, I think. For we were samples, and on their valuation of us would depend their reports on Kitchener's Army. The four of us aggregated about twenty-four feet four inches in length, and about fifty-three stone in weight, but I do not suppose they went much on that. General von Sanders had said to our youngest, "Eton? and Oxford?" and seemed pleased to find that his conjecture was right. He knew England well, and said that he had been in Ireland not long before the war. But the Turks were different. They looked at us a good deal, but ventured no overt guesses as to our antecedents. One Turkish officer, an Arab rather, and a descendant of the Prophet, as he told us, had lived in London, and spoke

English perfectly. Indeed, he boasted that in his veins there ran some drops of English blood, and told me the well-known family that had lent it. Being ignorant of the law of libel, I will not mention it here. He was a curious being. A violent Moslem, but not unfriendly to us personally. Indeed, he did me a real good turn, for he somehow or other sent a telegram for me to my wife and saved her from that awful anxiety that so many women have had to bear after receiving notice that their menkind were "missing."

I liked to listen to this friendly enemy's conversation. He had an idea that we had two submarines in the Sea of Marmora based upon the islands and supplied by the Greeks there.

It was impossible, he said, that our submarines should pass up and down the straits through all their nets and mines. But was it? Ask the E 7 or the E 11. Another favourite topic was the recuperative power of Islam. After this war, the Arab maintained, Turkey would recover much more quickly than the Western nations. "For," said he, "we are polygamous. We use the whole breeding power of our race, which resides in the women. Women are not being killed. They will all find husbands and bear children. We shall build up again our full power while you are still suffering from the deaths of your young men." There may be much truth in this. I think that all the enemy staff were very anxious at that time. They thought the Greeks had come in without declaring war, and one of my signallers, a short, dark man, a glass-blower from Yorkshire, had some difficulty in proving to the Turks that he was not a Greek. "Yok! Yok!" said the Turkish officer, "yok" being the Turkish for "no"; but he accepted the evidence of a pocketful of letters with English post-marks, and it probably saved the man's life—for the time—for he died of hard treatment two years later. I remember that this man said to me, "They say 'Yok, yok,' sir; they know they have got the East Yorks!" "Yok" was at that time the only Turkish word I knew, and that and "Yassak," meaning "forbidden," were the words I heard most often in Turkey.

The Turkish staff officers, even as the Germans, told us how hard they found it to get their allies to take prisoners. The fact was that they only went in for taking prisoners when they wanted to study our newly-landed forces. At all other times they murdered them. It is easy to demonstrate, as I think the following facts will show. On Gallipoli, I believe something like 700 officers and 11,000 men were posted as missing. Many of these were dead, of course, but certainly nothing like all. Of the 700 officers only 17 were taken prisoner, one in every forty-one; of the 11,000 men about 400 were taken prisoner, one in every twenty-seven. The details regarding the men I do not know, but the officers were taken as follows:—

At the first landing at Anzac	2
At Anzac when the August landing at Suvla Bay took place	2
At Suvla Bay from the 11th Division	5
Between Anzac and Suvla, at the same time, from the Ghurkas	1
At or in the region of Cape Hellas at the same time, from the 29th Division	3
At Suvla Bay, a few days later, when the Territorials landed	2
At Suvla Bay, again a few days later, from the Yeomanry	1
And one officer of the Australian forces was taken at the Anzac front when no new landing was on	1
	—
	17

That clearly shows that the prisoners were taken only to gain information as to the types of our new forces. But I have further evidence. I was one of four British officers who crossed the Sea of Marmora in a Turkish torpedo-boat, six days after we were captured. In the engineers' quarters with us was a sick Turkish officer, a Circassian, who spoke French. Of the four British, I happened to be the only one who could converse with him. He seemed pleased to see us, told us what a good time we should have in Constantinople; society, women, fine hotels, and other joys. We were extremely surprised. Then he told us that an order had come to take some prisoners, "and we have got some." We were again surprised, but polite, and conversation continued. Suddenly he said, "Who are you?" "British officers," I replied. "Oh!" he said, "I thought you were invalided Germans!"

Major-General Sir Charles Townshend has stated publicly since returning to England that the Turk is a sportsman and a clean fighter. This must have been said in complete ignorance of the whole series of damning facts which are now in the hands of our Government. I have brought out one of these facts, and others will appear as the book proceeds. Major-General

Townshend is to the best of my belief singular on this point among those officers, non-commissioned officers and men who were his fellow-prisoners in Turkey. The Turk is a master of the game he plays. A hospital-ship lying off the coast is secure from his artillery, because of the publicity, not because it is a hospital-ship. A wounded soldier behind a ridge, hid from the eye of the world's Press, has about as much chance with the Turks as he would have with a pack of wolves. An article I once read in a Turkish paper published in French, an article upon the damnable wickedness of the Entente, ended in these words: "C'est nous qui sommes les 'Gentlemen.'" They wish to play to the gallery of neutrals, and to pose as humane fighters. But they expected to win, and they thought the prisoners' stories would have to wait until after the war. We managed to evade this last wish of theirs; but of that later. It has been pointed out that the Turks did not use gas; indeed, they laughed at our respirators. I have heard, and I believe, that the true explanation of their reluctance was that they were found too unhandy and stupid to be trusted not to gas themselves.

There were good Turks; there are good wolves, for I have known one; but their rarity was above that of rubies.

There is one other question concerning Gallipoli which may fitly come into this chapter. I do not ask the question, but one of us four was asked it by General Liman von Sanders, and we did not then, and we do not now, know the reply. Von Sanders asked, "Why did General Hamilton send a handful like yours to attack the great hill that commands all my position. Did he think that I could be so blind as not to defend it against even a much stronger force?"

On the early morning of the 16th of August we reached the Quay of Stamboul.

CHAPTER II

CONSTANTINOPLE

WE were rather thankful to reach Constantinople. We crossed the Marmora by night in a rickety little torpedo-boat with something wrong with her screw, and we hoped to escape being sunk by one of our own submarines. The danger was a very real one, for it was only a few weeks after this that a Turkish transport with a number of British prisoners on board was sunk by one of our E-boats. But in that case they all escaped to barges alongside. We were sealed up like bully beef in a tin, and would have had no chance.

At the quay, our escorting officer left us. He bore the euphonious name of Fa'at Bey, but was not a bad fellow. And, unlike the majority of Turks, he had travelled and picked up a little English. Many Turkish officers speak French, and a few German; but knowledge of English is rare. What strikes one as very curious when first encountered is to find a Turk speaking English with a strong American pronunciation. The reason is that several very fine American colleges have been founded in Turkey, where first-class education is to be had cheaply. Later in our captivity we were so fortunate as to get to know the staff of one of these colleges very well, and nothing gives me greater pleasure than to pay some small tribute to their wonderful, unselfish work. But of that in another place.

From the quay we were driven in carriages through the streets of Stamboul, up the hill to the Ministry of War, and there confined in a fairly large room with blue-tiled embrasures and a very dirty floor. Heretofore we had lived in tents; we were now to begin our painful studies of Turkish domestic fauna.

Various Turkish officers came to see us; one tremendous swell, apparently made up to take a leading part in "Arms and the Man," was very impressive. He had the most complete appearance of gilded villainy that I have ever seen. He was the first, so far as I recollect, to play the favourite Turkish confidence trick upon us. It is a simple performance, and we were simple enough to be taken in by it—once. The procedure is thus:

Scene: Dirty room. Dirty prisoners in dirty clothes. Dirty beds. Dirty walls, covered with stains where former captives have squashed bugs. (Is that a filthy thing to write? I believe it is. But this is a history, and I shall have to write worse things than that.)

Enter. Gorgeous official, Interpreter with a mean, shifty face, and other incompetent perverts who look as though they were "walking on" for five piastres a performance. Probably they actually are.

Interpreter. "His Excellency wishes me to tell you that you are not prisoners, your country and mine are at war, but we are all soldiers. You are our honoured guests; is there anything that you require? All will be given you; in a few days you shall have complete liberty."

Senior Prisoner. "Please thank the—General, Pasha, Excellency, Bey, Effendi, or whatnot; the title does not affect the procedure—We should like to write letters, to have a bath, to have the beds disinfected, and to be able to purchase soap, tooth-brushes, underclothes, etc., etc."

Interpreter (after collusion with the great man): "Certainly, all these things will be allowed. Is there anything more you require?"

Prisoners make various suggestions.

Interpreter. "Yes, of course. You are our honoured guests. In one hour, perhaps."

Exeunt omnes, except prisoners.

And that is all. That is the whole trick. The keynote is the interpreter's final word "perhaps." Nothing whatsoever happens. The one hour spins out to many hours, to days, to months, to years. Nothing whatever comes of the interview. But in the course of time prisoners learn other means. Our "other means" in the Ministry of War was a cultivated person, the editor of a newspaper, who was serving in his country's army as a private soldier, and who had so far escaped fighting. He was put on to do us, and he did. But he did, at any rate, see that our meals were fairly regular, and he bought us tooth-brushes and a chess-board. Judged by the new standard we were fast assuming, he was not a bad fellow. I wonder to what extent it is a good thing to alter one's standards in that manner. Degradation of principles *versus* breadth of mind. It is one of the many undermining influences a prisoner has to combat if he would come back to the world a decent man.

The month was August, still warm, but with autumn and winter ahead of us. ONE autumn and winter, we thought. We had been captured in khaki drill, thin stuff only suited for tropical wear. So we were most agreeably surprised when our ex-editor caterer produced next day a Nubian person, a deserter of sorts from Egypt, who told us that he would procure us any clothes we required. Our total resources in actual cash were very small indeed, but the Nubian explained that our credit was enormous. Seldom have I felt such affinity to the international financiers. The lists we compiled were comprehensive and well chosen. The Nubian was as one taking an order from Rockefeller or Rothschild. The result was the usual one in Turkey. Nothing of all we had ordered ever appeared. I forget how many times this farce was repeated. If not four times it was at least as many as three. At this distance of time I will not affirm that the lists were identical each time; but at any rate the result was. So naked as we came into the world of official Stamboul, thus naked did we depart from it. And perhaps we were lucky to retain the clothes we had. Other prisoners at different times were robbed of their uniforms, more frequently of their boots, and among the men, poor fellows, many had at one time and another to sell their clothes to buy food. We did, at any rate, get out of that place with all we had brought in.

On the second day our numbers were doubled, for two officers of the Worcesters and two from the Australian Division joined us. They had been captured three days before our own misfortune, but had come the long way round from Gallipoli by road and rail. I know we looked at them as the bears in the Zoo might be expected to greet a new companion, but we soon settled down. About this time a batch of some 150 N.C.O.'s and men arrived, but we were not allowed to see them for several days. They were housed in very uncomfortable quarters below the level of the ground; bad enough, but not so bad as the awful room three naval officers occupied about a month later.

On one side of the Ministry there was a long, narrow garden, and as our room was a corner one we looked out both over the garden across the city and through the end windows. The view over the garden was magnificent. We could see a corner of the Bosphorus, and the buildings of Pera stretching away up the opposite hill-side. From the end windows there was a prospect in two stories, typical of the land of the Turk, a mixture of squalor and display. The upper storey was a very handsome grey stone mosque with four slender and very beautiful minarets, reaching up into the blue sky where birds for ever circled as emblems of the liberty we longed for. The lower storey was a paved courtyard with barred windows all along the side that faced us. From behind the bars came the voices of prisoners and the clank of chains, and through them we could see a mass of unfortunates either undergoing sentences or awaiting them; probably the latter; it is mostly waiting in Turkey. We used to see arms thrust out with small nickel coins in the hands to bribe their gaolers to fetch their owners food or cups of coffee. I remember one poor miserable wretch of an albino, with a face like a very, very thin Angora goat, who used to gibber through the bars all day long. He looked to me as though he had gone mad, and perhaps he had. Long afterwards I met a British prisoner who had been thrust in there among those ghastly creatures for a night, and from his account they were a queer lot.

In the garden there used to promenade a number of Turkish officers who apparently had nothing else to do. We thought, of course, that they were government servants passing away the time until pay-day came along once more. It was only a natural supposition; but it was completely wrong. They were, as a matter of fact, prisoners like ourselves. People who had infringed the Turkish military code, or had been convicted of swindles sufficiently considerable to entitle them to preferential treatment. In Turkey, an officer may be convicted of theft, but unless his sentence exceeds six months he suffers neither loss of his commission nor even loss of rank. And this is wise, for you could not have an army consisting of private soldiers only. Even in Russia they do not do that. So many of them were but biding the time until a benevolent system should again loose their energies to prove once more that charity begins at home. But some were of other categories. There was one who subsequently was so kind as to admit an Englishman into his confidence, and to explain how to remain an officer, with all its prestige and honour, while yet avoiding the more distressing features of war, such as wounds, danger, or even death. This officer, most meritoriously, had become a master of his country's military laws. A thing wholly to be admired in an officer. So skilled was he, and so fertile of resource, that he knew to a nicety the value of each crime. When war broke out he promptly committed one, was accused, awaited sentence, served it, and so escaped that tedious campaign in the frozen Caucasus. On being released, he selected from his repertory another crime, and bravely committed it, this time avoiding martyrdom in the Dardanelles. Similarly, he escaped the perils of that ill-judged attack on the Suez Canal, and, for aught I know, may at the very present moment be avoiding the infamy of seeing his country's capital city occupied by the infidel.

I did not mean to digress into Turkish law, but having done so I will go one step further in order to describe the procedure which is followed when a private soldier makes an accusation against an officer. My authority is the official interpreter who was for a time the bane of our lives at Afion-Kara-Hissar. On hearing the accusation, the senior officer determines what the sentence would be for that particular offence. Having done this justly and with an open palm, he arrests the accused and condemns him. The accused serves the sentence, whatever it may be—I believe one hundred and one years is the maximum for serious charges; and at the expiration of the penalty, the case is tried. The officer is then found either guilty or not guilty. If the former, he is politely informed that as he has already paid the price, probably in every sense of the word, he is now at liberty. The man who accused him is commended. If, on the other hand, he is found not guilty, he is reinstated in his former position, and the man who accused him wrongfully is beaten.

I cannot say whether this is a true description, but it is true that the interpreter told me this.

And, indeed, why should it not be true? Institutions as well as animals, even that greatest of animals, man, must subscribe to the natural law of the survival of the fittest. As already pointed out when describing the way in which a Turkish officer avoids loss of rank when convicted for theft, perhaps this arrangement is wise, in the circumstances; perhaps it fits those circumstances. For in the majority of cases a Turkish soldier is a more honest man than his officer, and in a high percentage of cases the accusation must be justified: in the remainder the officer is probably only paying the penalty of one of his undiscovered crimes.

What with the four new officers and the other ranks, we were by this time a considerable body, quite large enough to become the living illustrations of a national triumph. So, in due course, we were paraded in the square on the opposite side of the Ministry to our outlook, and were passed before a cinematograph. I do not remember how many times we circled round that infernal machine while the operator ground the handle, but it was a good many. By the time he had exhausted the roll of film we must have a very creditable appearance, several divisions at the very least. It was unfortunate for the Turks that they had not a captured gun to trundle round with us; but, even as it was, we have played a great part in the world.

At the end of the square, where it abutted upon the street, there was an arched gateway, something like a Roman triumphal arch, and in the room above it there resided an arch-villain. We had been in Constantinople about a week when we were commanded to his presence. He was a very great man indeed, popularly supposed to be Enver Pasha's remover-in-chief at a time when removals of political opponents were frequent. But we did not know that then; we only knew that he was a magnificent, tawdry and detestable person. That room lives in my memory as the gold and purple room. It was hung with velvet and decked with gilt, and the man sat in it like a frog in an orchid. We were given cigarettes, and were then informed that the British Government was ill-treating its Turkish prisoners so disgracefully that reprisals would have to be started. The infamous English, we were assured, made their Turkish officer prisoners march naked through the streets as a sport for the populace. What had we to say about it? Of course we denied the possibility of such a thing being true. But he remained unconvinced, of our knowledge, if not of our good faith. The interview left a sense of possible unpleasantness looming ahead of us.

The next day we received orders to move to a new barracks over in Pera.

When first in Turkey one is inclined to look upon all moves as desirable. Monotony and stagnation grow upon a prisoner very rapidly, and the first six months are much the hardest to bear. Any move rumoured or ordered shines like a light ahead. It must be an improvement, one thinks, it will in any case be an event, something to mark the passage of time. But after a year the average prisoner hates moves. By bitter experience he knows their cost and discomfort, the loss of his small, painfully-acquired property, and the trouble of settling down again. Also he knows that, much as he may hate the place he is in, there are many places worse. Still, we were at the beginning of things then, and we rejoiced in the move. We were marched down the streets of Stamboul, with our men, across the bridge over the Golden Horn, and up the steep street that leads to the top of Pera.

We passed on the way the small French hotel where I had stayed nearly eight years before, and listened to the howling of the dogs at night. The populace stared at us, but was not hostile. If any of them had seen the film of us in our thousands they must have been bitterly disappointed; or perhaps they thought it natural there should be so few survivors.

At the very top of the hill, where it bends down again towards the Bosphorus, we were led into the Taxim barracks. The men were given several large dormitories; the officers had a small room to themselves. This did not seem very bad. It was a smaller room than before, and it had no blue tiles, but otherwise not much worse. Our disillusion came with the fall of dusk.

That night we fought a battle.

We put up a tremendous struggle against impossible odds and we did not win.

When the sun set and the light in the room turned grey, forms were seen stealing down the walls, up the walls, out of the walls, and all over the walls; but mostly down the walls. Small, brown, flat creatures, easy to kill with anything hard, even with one's fingers. They began in tens, and ended in tens of thousands. And each one of every one of those thousands was a famished bug. Each one could wake a clean European by crawling over him, and keep him awake long after it was dead by the venom it injected into him. We were not very clean Europeans, but we were clean enough for that. We had not then acquired the stock of antibug-venene that we had in our veins later. We began by trying to slay them. We succeeded in slaying many hundreds, but their hosts were not perceptibly weakened, nor was their natural force abated. Moreover, they stank. A bug at large smells very noticeably, a bug squashed stinks. All that night we fought them unavailingly, and at dawn they drew their undiminished tribes away.

There were three nights like that, and seven of the eight of us hardly slept a wink the whole time. We slept a little by day. But had we stayed there long it would have been a hard fight for sanity. As it was, our nerves got very much on edge, and we were not the cheery companions we might have been. It may seem childish and hypersensitive to make a fuss about a few insects, but it was a very real horror; not only the actual itching, or even the odour, but there is something disgusting and degrading in being covered with beastly creatures of that sort, and I have heard pretty rough private soldiers say they felt the same when first afflicted by lice. "Private" was, I believe, originally short for "Private Gentleman," and the old meaning is not infrequently brought home to one.

Things were rather strained altogether in Taxim barracks. The Turkish guards were apt to be brutally rough with our men, despite our vigorous complaints. One solitary Frenchman there was too, a Corsican, and I saw a Turk kicking him most brutally on the floor one morning. There was very nearly a real explosion then, but the Turk stopped in time.

It was about this time that I began to realize what a very severe trial captivity would prove. It did prove so, and in ways I had not then foreseen. But it became apparent even then that work of some sort would have to be done if normality of mind were to be conserved. By the end of the war we had blossomed forth in all sorts of directions, but we were only feeling our way then.

Without saying or meaning one word against my fellow-prisoners, or even against myself, it must be clearly understood that first and foremost among the trials of captivity comes the unavoidable close proximity of other people. It is the prisoners themselves who are each other's principal discomforts. We were all so close to each other; so permanently in evidence to each other, and so different from one another that weariness of spirit grew to a pitch no outsider can comprehend. Bugs are bad, Turks are worse, but eternal neighbourhood is worse still. *Tout comprendre c'est tout pardonner*, but God alone reaches that "*Tout.*"

About the Taxim barracks there was one good thing. There is good in everything: in a bug it is his squashableness; in a Turk it is his stupidity; in Taxim it was the orchestra next door.

At the end of the narrow ground we were allowed to tread there was a sort of public garden, and in the afternoons the band played there. Twice we were conducted by a Turkish officer, a kindly old thing, to a bench facing this place of joys, and were allowed to watch the Levantine society that gathered there. We were even allowed to hail the waiter as he passed and have coffee handed up for ourselves and our janitor. It was a good time. We could hear music; we could watch children; and we could feel very nearly free.

Except for this narrow space, the grounds of Taxim barracks, so far as I observed, were a graveyard. Tall stones with carven turbans to indicate men's graves, flat stones for the graves of women, and gloomy cypress trees. And through the trees gleamed the Bosphorus.

CHAPTER III

THE ARMENIANS

AFTER three days of Taxim we were told that it had been decided to send us to Angora, where we would enjoy perfect liberty. None of us had a very clear idea where Angora was, but we knew it must be a pleasant change from Taxim.

There were not many preparations to make; no packing. My own luggage consisted, I remember, of a bit of soap, a tooth-brush, and a few other odds and ends, all contained in a paper bag tied up with a bootlace: the sort of bag you buy buns in. And I was one of the richest of the prisoners. I was rich in another respect, besides this wealth of luggage, although at that time I did not know it: for my prison hobby, art, industry, or whatever it may be called, had already started. For some reason or other the spirit moved me to write verses while a captive, and the first of all, a short poem entitled "Captivity" was written before we left Constantinople. This strange, and to me quite abnormal, habit endured for the whole of my thirty-nine months as a prisoner. It is good to have a pipe and tobacco in captivity, and it is good to have blankets, but it is even better than these to have an absorbing occupation.

We left Taxim early in the morning of the 25th of August and were ferried across the Bosphorus to Haida Pasha station. Technically speaking, we stood now for the first time in Asia, though, morally speaking, where the Turk rules there is Asia. We knew that Angora was a long journey: two days they told us, and it actually took thirty-six hours. But I think the vast size of Anatolia was rather a surprise to us all. In all ordinary atlases Asia Minor is shown on such a tiny scale that its hugeness is lost to mind.

Several officers and an armed guard accompanied us in the train, but only two individuals remain in my memory. One was a thick-set, short, fierce man of early middle age. He had one eye only, and his neck was almost circled by a frightful scar as though he had been operated upon by a blunt guillotine and then healed up again like the wolf in the fairy story who becomes a prince when you cut off his head. Only he had not gained the true, handsome, debonair appearance of a prince. He looked, and probably was, a very efficient murderer not yet on pension. His person bulged with lumps of muscle, daggers and pistols; and I am sure the interpreter meant to speak the truth when he told me that this ferocious person was one of the chiefs of the secret police. He was in charge of the party. The interpreter himself was the other member of our party who impressed me.

He travelled in the same compartment with us, and talked freely the whole way. He was the "Young Turk" complete, and ardent upholder of the Union and Progress party. When war broke out between England and Turkey he was in America, and he hoped to return there after the war. But, very patriotically, he came back to serve his country. He sailed in a Dutch ship, and touched at Plymouth on the way, where, he informed me, he went ashore under the guise of a Persian. He must, I think, have represented the mental attitude of his party very fairly. He was an undoubted patriot, and Turkey for the Turks was his keenest wish: but by the Turks he meant what is really a very small minority of the Ottoman tribe, and the other subjects of the Empire only concerned him as obstacles to be removed. He was the first person from whom we learned anything of the organised massacre of the Armenians then in progress. He told me that at Van the Turks had killed all the Armenians, men, women, and children; and he would agree to no condemnation of this dreadful act. "They were bad people," was his invariable reply. Nominally this man was a Mohammedan, whose feud with the Armenians had lasted for centuries, but actually he was an advanced Turkish freethinker, and, except perhaps subconsciously, I don't think religious feeling had anything to do with the bitterness he expressed. It was purely political. The Armenian is very much cleverer than the Turk, very stubborn, and impossible to assimilate. Turks of my acquaintance's kind look upon Armenians as an enemy race, a weed that must at all cost be eradicated. But his ambitions in the direction of destroying opposition to the Young Turk ideals did not stop with the slaughter of Christian subjects. Quite logically, from his point of view, he realised that the reactionary influence of the Old Turk party was an even more dangerous weed in the garden of progress than was Christianity. His hatred was directed particularly against the orthodox Mohammedans, and especially against the teachers and students of Islamic divinity. "When we have finished this war," he said, "we are going to kill all the Imâms. Their false teaching keeps the race from advancing."

I wonder if such people ever pursue their thoughts to an ultimate conclusion! After wiping out all who were not of their own way of thinking, there would remain a depleted race in a vast undeveloped territory where no immigrants would dare to settle, even if they were welcomed. All capital would be frightened away: labour would be scarce: and the strongest of their neighbours would swallow them up. At the time I knew no name for this intense feeling, this mental obsession. But in the light of time it now looks like pure Bolshevism.

It seems that I have drawn a very revolting character. But the interpreter's was not wholly that. On the whole, he was the best man I met among the many interpreters who dealt with us during the next three years. He was fond of some of the beautiful things of life, a lively critic of literature, a reader of poetry, both English and Turkish, and, from his own account, a personal friend of those among his compatriots who were foremost in striving to rouse their countrymen to intellectual endeavour. I loathed the man's ideas but rather liked the man. It seemed that he suffered from the absorption of a wrong tone; almost from a disease of the soul, but an infectious disease, not an innate deformity: a calamity of environment, not of heredity. There was something exceedingly sad in the picture he drew of a great national effort going hopelessly astray because its ideals were false. But he did not see that the picture was sad. He thought it glorious.

For the first part of the journey we skirted the Sea of Marmora, along the flanks of bare hills, now tunnelling through promontories, and now looking down upon blue bays. There were trenches dug all along the coast, and armed guards at every bridge and culvert. Far away, to the south-east, we saw forest-covered hills. Then the line turned inland, past the town and lake of Ismid, through a valley of orchards where the apples were almost breaking the trees, and up into the foot-hills. This part of Anatolia is exceedingly fertile wherever the slopes are not too steep to dig. But the hills are very barren, only fit for the most part for the nomad life of the Turkish sheep- and goat-herds. We travelled through hills and valleys all that afternoon, and by dusk had begun the climb that leads up to the great plateau of Asia Minor. The railway followed the line of a river up the valley it had cut through the hills. Followed it up until it became a stream, and followed it on until it became a rushing mountain torrent crossed and recrossed by the line.

When dawn broke the engine was panting up the last few miles of the incline, and we ran out into a wide land of rolling downs and farm country, three thousand feet above the level of the sea. Having lived in mountains before I foresaw a very cold winter.

It was not very long after this that we began to see the Armenians.

As everyone knows now, the late summer and the autumn of 1915 saw organised, State-supported massacre of the Armenians carried out in Turkey on a scale unknown previously in modern history, perhaps unparalleled in all history. I shall not attempt any comprehensive account of this national crime, for the whole story is already contained in the blue book on the subject, printed by the British Government, and edited by Viscount Bryce. Those who wish to hear the details of how somewhere about one million men, women and children were outraged, tortured and done to death can refer to that book. I will only say that the many isolated facts gathered from many sources during my three years in Turkey all piece together in that book so completely that no doubt exists in my mind regarding its truth. The blue book is a sincere and unexaggerated statement of fact, not a propaganda war book. It rings true from beginning to end.

The first sight we had of the Armenians who were being deported was a large straggling camp of women and children close beside the railway line. We had no idea at the time that their men folk were already dead, or that they were almost all doomed to death or domestic slavery. It looked merely like a very large, very ill-organised gypsy encampment. Those women and children were awaiting trains to convey them hundreds of miles from their homes into the most inhospitable regions of Asia Minor. Ahead of them they had days of travel in trains, camps where the girls would be sorted out again and again until only the ugliest were left; and, at the end, a march where nearly all of them would die from fatigue. For the Turkish way is to drive, on and on, wearily on, until almost all are dead. They did it to the Armenians in 1915, and in 1916 they did it to the captured garrison of Kut-el-Amara.

We passed several trainloads of these wretched refugees. They were in trucks mostly, terribly overcrowded, and some of them were in sheep trucks in two stories, the lower tier only able to crouch.

The interpreter told me they were being sent to a very hot district where they could do no harm. "They are bad people," he added.

There were a few boys among them, and a few old men. The rest had been murdered.

Englishmen don't like Armenians. I don't myself. Turks loathe them. Greeks dislike them. In the Caucasus the Georgians hate them. This almost universal unpopularity is no excuse at all for massacre, but—in Turkey—it helps to explain it. Where the European avoids, the Turk, having a different standard, slays. To him they are vermin. Here is a story told by an Armenian woman to a British officer. It is the story of a "good Turk"; the expression was the woman's, not the officer's. There was a batch of Armenian women and girls driven on until their drivers grew weary that they would not die. Sick at heart they grew of the perpetual driving of these weeping creatures. There were no pretty ones left, for the most comely will lose their pitiful beauty when starved long enough. So there was no interest left in being their custodians. The drivers grew to hate the work, for there was no end to it, and no reward. So they were herded together and slain. But two survived, a woman and her daughter. They hid among the corpses and remained there until the corpses began to crawl. The corpses of their friends and relations. They had to leave that place, and in great fear they stole away by night. There were a few Turkish villages not far away, and in the morning they met a Turk. This was the good Turk of the story. He stopped them and asked who they were, and they told him. "Come with me," he said to the girl, "and I will feed you." So the girl followed him to his house, and the mother followed too, though she was not invited. They reached the house and the Turk went inside. He came out with his gun. "I do not want the old woman," he said, as he shot her. But to the girl he gave food, and did not ill-treat her, for he was a good Turk.

Why do these people hate the Armenians so much?

I think it is partly because the Armenian is usually a successful merchant, outclassing the Turk in commerce, competing on more than equal terms with the Greek, and at least rivalling the Jew. But it is chiefly because the Armenian race has been ground under the heel of a people naturally their inferiors for so many centuries. It is a survival of the fittest, and it is the Turks who have made the conditions which the survivors have had to fit. The whole race has been moulded by the hand of the Turk. For centuries he has slain all those who displayed the more manly virtues. He has been like a breeder of sheep who hated black sheep but feared white. For centuries he has slain the white but contemptuously allowed many of the black to survive. Unconsciously he has been a selective breeder on a very large scale; and he has bred the modern Armenian. If we ourselves, we British who are so proud, had passed through those dark centuries with the Armenians, we too would be like they are, or not much otherwise. If the Armenians are protected; allowed to be successful and to enjoy their success themselves; allowed to be independent and not suffer for their independence; allowed to be brave and not to die for their courage; allowed, in a word, fair play, they will grow into a fine people.

When the great massacres took place there was, among the Armenians, one strange exception to the universal peril. Most Armenians belong to the Armenian Church, but a certain number of them are Roman Catholics. I do not know what happened elsewhere, but in Angora the Roman Catholic Armenians were not killed, or deported, which is the same as being killed only slower. They were not well-treated, but they did survive.

It is a very remarkable thing to find the power of Rome exerted in so wonderful a way in a Mohammedan country. And were this the only example of it one would be inclined to attribute the influence to some local predilection. But there are two other instances. One was a division of the prisoners, French and British, by which the Roman Catholics were sent to a camp where there was at that time considerably more liberty. The other was quite extraordinary: it was the repatriation of a British officer who happened to be the nephew of a cardinal. We did not grudge him his good luck. He stole no march on us. But it certainly was a most wonderful piece of fortune for him. He was not ill or injured, and he was not exchanged, but simply repatriated. He gave his parole, and that was all.

In contrast to the present-day power of the Pope in Turkey it is interesting to remember that a large percentage of the Jews who are subjects of the Ottoman are the descendants of Spanish Jews who fled into the Sultan's dominions to escape from the Spanish Inquisition. Many of them still speak Spanish. They are not often ill-treated by the Turks, I believe, though how they manage to avoid it is a miracle.

We reached Angora long after dark and were met by a Bimbashi who conveyed us in carriages to our new quarters. The men marched, but to the same destination, and it was after our arrival there that we were able for the first time to talk with them freely. This was seventeen days after capture.

We drove through the squalid streets of a corner of the town, and out about a mile into the country. I think we all shuddered as we drew near a large barrack and remembered Taxim, and breathed more freely when we had left it behind. Our destination was not a particularly sweet place, but it was better than that.

We crossed a bridge, passed a mulberry plantation, and the carriages halted at the foot of a slope leading up to a group of buildings surrounded by a high wall. A small, low, iron-studded door, guarded by a sentry with a fixed bayonet, was opened. We stooped through it, walked beneath an arched gateway, and came out in a paved courtyard surrounded by buildings black against the starry sky. As we came in heads popped out of the windows, and we heard people speaking in French. That sounded civilized at any rate. Have you who read this ever considered what the word "civilized" means? It means a good deal when you are in the middle of Anatolia. Through a door to the left and up a flight of steps we went, and at the top we were met by three French naval officers, headed by Commander Fabre, who welcomed us so courteously and kindly that my heart warms to think of it to the present day.

Everything that a fellow-prisoner could do they had done. And when the Turks had gone and the gate was locked once more, we sat down with them to an excellent meal.

Our friends were the officers and crew of the submarine "Mariotte," sunk in the Dardanelles rather more than a month before. Two of the officers spoke English fluently, and the third was a dogged striver who had mastered a great deal of our language before the end of the war.

From them we learned what this strange building was. It was called the Wank (pronounced Wonk) and was an Armenian monastery, half farm, half stronghold. What had happened to the monks they did not know, save that they had been turned out. As a matter of fact they were dead. Very nearly everything they had had been moved by the Turks, looted by officials and officers, but we came into joint possession with the French of a few beds; enough for the officers, the men were not allowed beds; a divan round three sides of a fairly comfortable room, a shower-bath, and some framed photographs of various high dignitaries of the Armenian Church. There were also lamps and a stove. This was a very great advance on any home we had yet had in Turkey; for, although a European housekeeper would have been disgusted at the vermin, they were not sufficiently numerous to keep one awake all night.

We found, too, that the French had managed to establish the custom of taking in a newspaper, "The Hilal," a German edited, Levantine rag, which did, at any rate, publish the German *communiqués*. So we began once more to look upon the war and the outside world through that dim glass which was our only window. Later on we had various other means, but not up till then.

In addition to the large central sitting-room, where four of us had to sleep, there were three small bedrooms on the same floor, also a kitchen, a latrine, and a tiny paved room where the shower-bath hung. This was an amateur one made out of a kerosine oil tin, and its existence argued virtue in one Armenian at least. The Turks had not stolen it. It was of no use to them.

Derrick and I, who had been taken together, were now in a mess of eleven persons, quite a sizeable community. We began to wake up and make plans to learn French and to teach English; but that night we slept like logs.

CHAPTER IV

THE WANK

WE had now a breathing space. We had reached the place where the Turks meant to keep us, and though we had yet to learn that Turks never continue to follow the same policy for very long, we now had time to settle in as comfortably as circumstances permitted.

Our space was strictly circumscribed. There was the series of rooms already described as belonging to the officers, and there was the paved courtyard, perhaps thirty yards square. This was common to the officers and about 150 N.C.O.'s and men. Officers were not allowed to visit the men's dormitories. On the east side of the courtyard was a church, locked up and sealed. Through its windows we could see that a quantity of books were stored there. On the north were further monastic buildings in two stories. We were not allowed upstairs, but the men were allowed the use of a kitchen on the ground floor. The western side consisted of a few sheds and a high wall, and the southern side held all the rooms occupied both by officers and men. These were all two-storied buildings.

The Wank being built on a hill-side with the ground falling away to the south, the officers' quarters got no sunshine, for their only window which looked in that direction was in the landing at the head of the stairs. From there we could see the town of Angora covering its steep hill, and crowned by a great rambling castle. Below the southern window there was a second courtyard, into which a wide gate opened, which was apparently used as a pen for the monastic flocks at night; and below that again was a third yard, probably used as a pound for their cattle. The whole group of buildings and yards was surrounded by a high wall.

One very marked feature of the Wank was its awful smell. In Turkey there are drains, but they are perhaps worse than none at all. I shall not attempt to describe this disgusting feature of all the houses in Asia Minor I have ever been in, further than to mention that the cesspool is invariably buried underneath the house itself, preferably beneath the kitchen floor. It is, as a rule, ill-made of rough stone masonry. Further comment is unnecessary.

There were several curious relics of antiquity in the courtyard we frequented: a Greek inscription on one of the stones of the pavement; the carven tombs of several abbots, with mitres on their heads and croziers in their hands; and a very large stone head of a man or a god with thick, curly hair and a beard. It might have been a head of Jupiter, and probably came from one of the old Roman temples of Angora; unless, as is not improbable, the Wank itself stood upon the site of some more ancient religious foundation. The buildings we lived in were less than a century old, but the church appeared to be very much older.

The men had little to complain of while they were here. Their food was not particularly good, but it was not inadequate for men who could get no exercise. The only ill-treatment they had received was being robbed of their boots while on the peninsula, and they now appeared in every form of Turkish footgear, from rough army boots to thin slippers. When they began to travel again those were lucky who had boots.

The Turkish Government fed the men, but the officers were supposed to cater for themselves. One of the French officers who had already picked up a few words of Turkish acted as mess secretary, and a chaous, or Turkish sergeant, used to make purchases in the town for us. We had orderlies to cook and clean up.

Things were extraordinarily cheap then. The war had not yet affected country places like Angora, and paper money had not yet come into circulation. When it did so, gold and silver first, and copper and nickel next disappeared entirely from the shops and bazaars; and before I left Turkey a golden pound would purchase six paper pounds, while the exchange for silver was little lower. But at first things were cheap, and we managed quite well on our four shillings a day.

Some explanation of the system of supporting officer prisoners is necessary. The British Government refused to pay Turkish officer prisoners at the rate of pay given to equivalent British ranks. This was the old convention, but it could not be carried out with a country like Turkey, where the rates of pay were so much lower than ours. So Turkish officer prisoners were given 4s. a day for subalterns and captains, while field officers got 4s. 6d. But, in addition to this, Turkish prisoners were catered for at wholesale contract rates, were given firing, light, beds and bedding, as well as all necessary furniture. They were, for prisoners, exceedingly well off. I know this for a fact, for on my release I went over the P. of W. camp near Alexandria and saw their arrangements. The Turkish followed suit in refusing to give us the Turkish pay of our equivalent ranks, substituting for it the same rates as were given by the British, viz., 4s. 6d. and 4s. a day. But they did not give us any of the other necessaries of life. While in the Wank, it is true, we made use of the Armenian furniture, but that was for a very short time; and elsewhere in Turkey, for the next three years, British officer prisoners had to make or purchase every single thing they required—beds, tables, chairs, blankets, firewood, lamps, oil; everything. My share of fuel alone for the last winter in Turkey cost me £Tq.40 in a mess of twelve.

Very, very rarely we got Government issues of raisins, sugar, and soap at Government rates. Sometimes we got bread at Government prices, and occasionally firewood. But the general rule was that we fended for ourselves on our four bob, and competed in the open market. Had it not been for the help extended to us by the protecting Ambassador—first American and later Dutch—things would have gone very hard with us. As I mentioned a page or two back, the metal money disappeared and paper sank to one-sixth of its face-value. At the same time, prices soared to such a pitch that, at the end, a suit of clothes cost £Tq.100 (the Turkish sovereign is nominally worth about 18s. 6d.), a pair of boots cost £Tq.40, a quilt cost £Tq.15, tea about £Tq.16 per lb., and everything else in like proportion. But our income remained unaltered in nominal value. For the first three months we were paid in gold, and thereafter in paper. And at the end of the war we were receiving the same number of pounds *per mensem* in paper as we had received at the beginning in gold. It follows that a deduction of four shillings a day made in England by the paymaster produced for us a sum of four shillings a day divided by a factor which gradually rose to be six. One-sixth of four shillings is 8d. It was fortunate for us that our Government and the protecting Embassies realized the position. Even as it is, the loss has been not inconsiderable.

This excursion into the realms of finance is not meant as a complaint, but it seemed to me necessary to explain how we managed things.

For the first few weeks in the Wank we had no further glimpse of the outside world. In Angora one night there were a number of shots fired, and the next day two or three people were buried in the graveyard outside the walls. That is about the only event I can remember. Probably it was the aftermath of the massacres. The Turkish officer in charge of us used to come nearly every day. He had been a prisoner himself once, in Russia, for he had taken part in the famous defence of Plevna about thirty-six years before. He was of the old school, and found it rather hard to understand why prisoners taken in a holy war should be kept alive at all. Certainly he failed to understand that they had any further rights or privileges. He was irksome to deal with, and abominably pigheaded, also he swindled us, but I don't think he disliked us personally. His extraordinary and characteristically Turkish denseness of perception was his worst fault, and he was a great deal pleasanter than the slimy rogue who succeeded him. His attitude was simply this: "What! the prisoner demands something! Damn the prisoner, he is lucky to be alive! If I feel like being kind, I will." And he not infrequently was kind. But with an omnipotent person of this kind in charge of one, possessing life only, it takes some time and much friction to gain a few privileges to make that life worth having.

The old fellow had a fad of teaching us Turkish at one time. He used to call us into the room with the settees round it, sit down at a table, and begin to exchange languages with us. As we knew nothing of his, and he nothing of ours, while there was no common tongue to bridge with, this was slow work. "Ben," he would shout, and prod his chest with his finger. "Ben," we would all reply, and point at him. Then he would go off into something infinitely complex, shouting louder than ever, and by the end of the lesson we would have learnt, not that his personal name was Benjamin, but that "Ben" is the Turkish personal pronoun, first person singular. But these lessons did not endure for long. We all got sick of them.

I have racked my brains to think what else we did in those dull weeks, but almost in vain. The gramophone records in my convolutions were so badly scratched that I can hardly decipher a line of them. Chess I remember, for Fabre and I used to play most evenings, and we taught some of the others. I remember reading the paper to the men in the yard. I also remember two awful rows, things inevitable among prisoners, one English and one French. The English row was personal and particular, it culminated in a friendship that will endure. The French row was political, about Caillaux, and they talked so fast that there was a distinctly visible rainbow round the two principals. It did not culminate at all.

Those few things, and stinks, are actually all that I can call to mind.

How wonderful a siren is memory! As a boy at Winchester I suffered untold pangs. This much is an intellectual conviction to me. Yet it is all set in a golden haze of distance, and there are few pleasures I prize more than to return there. And if I have a son he shall go there, where his father, and my father, and his father and grandfather went. And he will suffer the same pains that they all suffered, and will remember as little of them as I do and they did. To-day is the 15th of April, 1919, and already memory has weeded out the pains of that dolorous year, 1915, to a very great extent. In course of time, in second or third childhood, I shall look back to Angora with tears of joy, and wonder why I did not settle there.

But things did begin to happen at last, and the first of them was that we obtained the privilege of promenading for an hour in the afternoon along the bank of the little stream that flowed in the bottom of the valley. There were willow trees there, and we used to peel their branches and make walking sticks carved with snakes, regimental badges, and other rivalries to Grinling Gibbons.

We used to watch the ants, too, and I regret to say that we used to feed them to the ant lions. Fabre was a notable athlete, a Hercules in miniature, and he used to run and jump. But all the time sentries stood round, armed to the teeth, and we were not really free. How the Wank did smell when we got back!

Then something really important occurred, for a new Army Corps Commander came to Angora, and he was a gentleman. His name was Chukri Bey, and I remember it as that of a man of honour. He was an Arab, not a Turk.

The first time he came it was in state, and he made a personal inspection of that awful drain and gave orders to abate the nuisance. The second time he came it was alone on a surprise visit. Again he made a personal inspection, and great was his wrath that nothing had been done.

After this we got much more liberty and better treatment all round, but that I will describe later.

And soon after this another important thing happened, for some more prisoners arrived, six officers among them. They were established higher up on the hill-side, in a temporarily disused agricultural college; and after a few days we met.

Rather an amusing incident occurred on their journey up, which I am sure they will forgive my repeating. They had been kept separate in Constantinople, the three naval officers in an underground dungeon, and the three military officers elsewhere. The first time they were brought together was in the train; and evidently the Turkish authorities expected them to unburden themselves to each other. Fortunately, they were too wise. Among their escort was the one-eyed ruffian I have already described, and their interpreter was a guileless youth who spoke French fluently but not a word of English. To wile away the time, they proceeded to teach this youth English verses, which he repeated after them. By considerable endeavour he became word perfect in a rhyme all about a ruddy sparrow and a ruddy spout together with the sparrow's adventures therein. Reasonably ribald people will perhaps recognize the schoolboy doggerel. All this the interpreter faithfully recited, and they told him it was one of the best known works of the famous William Shakespeare. When they were safely housed in their new quarters the interpreter came to see us, and he spoke the most perfect English! He had been planted on them as a listener. It is hard justly to apportion the honours. But I think that interpreter should have a future on the stage.

It was not long after this that we lost two of the French officers. The Turkish Government used, about twice a month, to make laborious lists of us, and presumably to lose them again. In these were entered our names, our father's names, our birthplaces, our religions, and some dozen other useless details. It was a slow business, and the transliteration of English names into Turkish script was not always quite satisfactory as will be conceded when I mention that a French speaking Turkish doctor once transfigured my name into TCHARLISTRI. But in it all there was some idea which we had not grasped; for suddenly they informed us that all Roman Catholics were to be transferred to a place called Afion-Kara-Hissar, a place stated to be more desirable than Angora. One of the French officers was a Protestant, but he was torn ruthlessly from the bosoms of the others, and the R.C.'s were dispatched to Afion. We were very sorry to lose them, and the unfortunate Protestant was exceedingly miserable at having to stop behind.

A few days later all the Protestant non-commissioned officers and men were ordered off to a place two days' march over hills to the north, Changri by name. Many of them had only thin slippers to walk in, and their bad times began from then, poor fellows. Their bones lie along the highways of Asia Minor, where they built roads and tunnels for their captors, yoked in a slavery as complete as any could be.

We could do nothing at all to help. We gave them what we could to set them forth, and never saw most of them again.

At the last moment, just when they were starting, it was discovered that they were two short. They had been counted wrongly. Turks find it hard to count beyond the number of their fingers and toes which number is the same as with human beings. This was a horrible dilemma. Red tape demanded x men, and the officer in charge could only produce x-2. But even as a ram in a thicket was sent to Abraham when about to sacrifice Isaac, so did the god of Anatolia provide even for this emergency. At this time two sick French sailors returned from hospital. They were only just convalescent: they were Roman Catholics; they were expected at Afion-Kara-Hissar. But all this was of no avail, and the poor protesting fellows were sent off with our poor British.

After they had departed the Wank seemed empty and lonely. We now explored it through and through, but found nothing of interest. The trees were changing their colour; the evenings drew in and grew cold. We became acutely aware that on this upland, winter would be very severe, perhaps terrible. Firewood became a problem, and, to feed the stove, we began to pull pieces off the more easily detachable parts of the Wank. It had to be done quietly, and long planks had to be dodged past the sentries; but we managed to have fires.

Then there came a real change. The Army Corps Commander decided to give us very much more liberty. Sentries' faces changed with the times; even the old veteran of Plevna began to realize that prisoners were human beings, and life grew bright once more. Accompanied by guards with sidearms only we used to visit the town and the shops, and we began to explore the neighbouring country. It was all hills, range behind range of hills; a most difficult country to travel through without good maps or a guide. Just over the hill behind the Wank there was a valley full of little farms; nice houses with vineyards attached. But all were empty, except such as were full of Turkish soldiers. They had been owned by Armenians, and their owners had gone, never to return.

Another place that we were free to explore at this time was the cemetery which lay on the east of the Wank. It was not without interest, for most of the tombstones had been filched from some Roman or Byzantine ruin, and still bore many traces of their former adornment. The great majority bore inscriptions in Armenian characters which we could not read; but, among them we found to our surprise quite a number of European graves. There were several Danes buried there, a few Frenchmen, and half a dozen British, Scots for the most part. The earliest of these, so far as I recollect, was that of a certain William Black, Mercator Angliæ, who had died at Angora in the year 1683 A.D. I have often wondered what brought old William Black so far afield, and whether he was the ancestor of any of the red-haired children we used occasionally to see in the town. We had a theory that it was he who had taught the inhabitants how to make shortbread, for there was a bare-legged boy who used to hawk shortbread in a glass box along the streets of Angora.

So in small things we found great interest, as prisoners do. Almost every day we used to see Turkish recruits training. They were a sturdy lot of rough young countrymen, splendid material either for war or peace, if only their Government were not so corrupt and inefficient. For the most part they were armed with sticks cut from the willows by the stream, and with these rude substitutes they had to learn the beginning of their drill.

The knowledge they acquired was literally kicked into them by the chaouses, brutal ruffians trained on the Prussian model. I have seen one of them haul a man out of the ranks, box his ears first on one side and then on the other, and then turn him round and kick him savagely. The recruit would stand it all stolidly, and salute before he returned to the ranks. In the evening parties of recruits who had been training out on the hills used to march back to barracks past the Wank, singing their marching song, a simple thing with a very primitive tune to it, said to have come into popularity at the time of the last Bulgarian war.

Some time in October a festival drew near, a public holiday called Kurban Bairam. The troops were to have a great sham fight, and sports were to be held. Chukri Bey, the Army Corps Commander, very kindly invited us to attend, and we stood behind him to watch the sham attack develop. He was a fine figure of a man and a splendid horseman. When the troops were drawn up preliminary to the show he rode at full gallop along their line, turned, rode back to the centre and pulled up short. Then he made a speech, no word of which we could understand, and they all cheered.

The attacking force marched off, and we took up our positions behind the defenders of a low abrupt ridge. Just on our left I remember there was a man with a stick and a kerosine oil tin doing machine-gun. The grey lines advanced from among the distant willows, attacked right across the open, and apparently won the day. They were as full of the fun of it as children playing at soldiers. Chukri Bey then made another speech, pieces of which he translated in French for us, and the show was over.

I have fought in the Great War, but that is the only sham fight I have ever seen in my life, for my training was marred by a period in hospital.

The next day was the sports, and we were given good seats in the official enclosure, just behind the Army Corps Commander and the Vali—the Governor of the Province. Chukri Bey continually turned round and explained things to us in French. He had made arrangements for two or three of our men who had been left behind in hospital to have seats in a good place. We saw the Turk at his best that day. His hospitality, his simplicity, his tough, rugged endurance were all to the fore. And we owed the whole of it to Chukri Bey. When, soon afterwards, he was sent elsewhere, we realised how rare a character his was among enemy officers. He was an Arab and we were told that his wife was an Egyptian princess.

One of the items was a football match played by schoolboys, and four British officers were invited to take part. Two played on either side. Games followed, rather like the games that children play at village school-feasts in England, bearing to those the same resemblance that baseball does to mixed rounders. Then there was some bayonet fighting, one of the rules of which was that the winner of a bout had next to take on two opponents simultaneously. A very up-to-date Turkish officer, girt with stays, and beautiful beyond the power of words, condescended to engage the winner in sword v. bayonet. I don't think he was very seriously pressed. The bayonet fighting was quite amusing to watch, but the great item of the day was the wrestling. All competitors, and there were about forty of them, strolled out into the arena and stretched themselves. They mingled together, and moved slowly about looking for mates, like young men and girls at a seaside place. Apparently anyone could challenge any other. Then there came a preliminary hug, in which each in turn just lifted his adversary off the ground, seemingly like our boxers' handshake, to show there is no ill-feeling. After which they fell to, and wrestled until one was beaten. Often there were half a dozen pairs struggling at one and the same time.

Some of the grips were very severe; a favourite method was to reach along each other's arms and seize each other's breasts, digging in their fingers like claws. It looked as though it must hurt horribly, but these hardy men seemed to enjoy it. One of the best was a negro, but the champion was a Turk. At the end Chukri Bey gave away prizes, simple and useful articles, no gold medals or silver cups; a pair of socks, a tobacco box, a knife, and a pleasant word for each winner.

It was not long after this that our sojourn in the Wank came to an end. The building was wanted as a barrack, and they wished to have us more safely housed in the town itself. So one fine day we were moved into Angora, and housed temporarily in a Greek hotel.

CHAPTER V

ANGORA

THE town of Angora is built round a hill. Originally there was a large castle on the top of the hill, with walls conforming to the rocky nature of the site, and outside the castle a walled town. The walls still remain, but the town has burst its bonds and overflowed down the slopes and out on to the plain below. At many points among the rocks, at all levels, springs gush out, and this water is very clear and good, a thing that Orientals attach great value to. The walls themselves are full of interest. When they were built, and whether by Byzantine Greeks or by the Turks themselves, I do not know. But they contain innumerable fragments of an earlier civilization. There are sculptured figures which once ornamented Roman altars, the capitals of Greek pillars, very many inscriptions in Greek and Latin, and a number of carved stones stolen from the fine marble temple of Augustus which still rears high walls near the bottom of the town. So beautifully was this temple built that it still defies the efforts of those who would destroy it in order to mend their houses with its marble blocks. A mosque is built against its wall, and the cornice is built on by the storks, but the temple still preserves much of beauty. Higher up in the town, one of the Turkish mosques carries its roof on Roman pillars; and wherever you go in the town there are traces of olden days.

On three sides the town flows down into the valleys round it, but the fourth side is one wall of an almost precipitous gorge, where a stream has cut through the range, and separated off this hill for men to build on. The place has the usual legend of a secret passage connecting the castle with the neighbouring hill. Afion-Kara-Hissar, too, has the same legend; and I have found it generically wherever rocks have been crowned with castles, in many lands. At the bottom of the gorge is the evil-smelling quarter of the skinners and tanners, men who proved their value when it was resolved to slay the Armenians.

From very early times, indeed, Angora must have been occupied. It is well supplied with water, very defensible, and situated at the junction of great caravan routes which penetrate northwards to the Black Sea and eastwards, through Sivas, to the Caucasus. In the plain to the north-west of the town there are barrows much like those on Salisbury Plain.

Many battles have been fought in the plain before Angora, and the city has often been sacked and burnt.

No place I have ever known has such an atmosphere of evil history looming in its streets. Should some prophet (or is it profit?) of psychometry venture to sleep there, she would probably die in horrible agony.

Even to the present day Angora is a great rendezvous of caravans. When we were there it was still the terminus of the railway stretching out toward central Asia, and we used to see long strings of laden camels approaching the town from far away. They pass with silent step along their wide, worn routes, tied in strings of four or five, each one's nose to the saddle of the one ahead, and with a donkey to lead the procession. They looked as if they had walked straight out of the Old Testament, and many of the men with them looked much more like what the Patriarchs must have been than the benevolent old gentlemen in stained glass windows can do.

Kurds we used to see, and Turks, and men of tribes we could not place. Generally they wore huge astrakhan hats of black, curly lamb's wool, and as a rule their broad belts were stiff with daggers and pistols, with generally a rifle slung across their shoulders as well. I often used to think what a wonderful experience it was for our untravelled men to see these strange people from the back of beyond. Strings of camels used to penetrate the dim, winding lanes of the city, and nasty, snarling, tusky creatures they were to dodge about among. But the real gathering place of the caravans was a trampled space of many acres which lay out beyond the railway station. A Golgotha it was, a place of skeletons and skulls. For centuries, for millenniums, perhaps, it had been the place where men and camels met and exchanged the news of Asia, mostly of wars and rumours of wars, of invasions, murders, massacres, the sack of cities, and tales of brigands in the hills. For all these mountain roads are infested by armed bands, even to the present day.

In the town itself there are two or three fairly good streets, paved with cobble-stones, and flanked by small boutiques, but most of the streets are narrow gullies; steep, winding, and dim. The houses have usually stables on the ground floor, while the stories above project and shut out the light; so much so that it is quite a feature of these thread-like lanes to find each house built with one shoulder thrust out, facing half-right one side of the street, half-left the other, and enabling the windows to collect some of the light which falls along the lane.

I think, between us, we explored the whole town. Under Chukri Bey's benevolent *régime* we had almost complete liberty, very much more than a prisoner could expect. Save that we had to be accompanied by guards, we were free to wander where we would, in the town and out of the town. We used to go shopping in the covered bazaar, where whole streets were shut up, their owners murdered. We used to explore the castle, and climb its crags. We used to take walks down the valley among the irrigated vegetable gardens. We used to walk among the hills. And through those hills some of us intended one day to walk to the sea. Not now, but in the spring.

The people were not at all hostile to us. I think they rather liked us. We used to shop a great deal. Our power to buy was limited only by our purse. But we used to shop for hours, like a pack of women in Kensington, all shopping no buying. For we had practically no money, and we had not only to buy blankets and clothes for the winter, but also to set up house, buy crockery, cutlery, cooking pots. Four bob a day, even when it still is four bob, is not much to set up house on. So we shopped much but bought little. There was a large store in the main street, run by Spanish Jews, and we used to swarm in there in a gang. A very funny sight we must have been, dressed all sorts of ways, some of us with shorts on, one young Australian, I remember, wore long pink drawers under and below his shorts and a fur cap on his head. For we wore the headgear of the country. We were advised to, to avoid exciting too much attention; and some of us wanted to acquire a set of disguise. Personally I had no other headgear of any kind, except a sort of Glengarry made of pieces of puttee stitched together. My helmet had been lost soon after I was captured. But the townsfolk did not seem to think us strange. They were remarkably polite. Several officers out for a walk one day met a man with a shot-gun, and asked to be allowed a shot. He handed over the gun; they tossed for the shot; a naval officer won, put up a woodcock and killed it.

Who, then, it may be asked, were the murderers, the people who killed about a million Armenians and quite a lot of Greeks? Well, just anybody and everybody. A Turkish peasant with a plough in his hand is a generous, open-hearted, simple fellow. A Turkish peasant with a gun in his hand is a brigand. The lower orders of the town are straightforward, simple people, but come a massacre, and they take their part. Probably things in France were not a bad parallel at the great St. Bartholomew's Eve. And it must always be remembered that the great drive of the Armenians was a Government affair, a national policy. Turks cannot stand having power. A private soldier who becomes an N.C.O. becomes, nine times out of ten, a black-guard. An ordinary citizen who becomes an official becomes, ten times out of ten, a thief. A common man who is invited to kill his Christian neighbour, free of all danger of punishment, does so. Throughout captivity the guards were faithful mirrors of the powers above. In the time of Chukri Bey they were kind, faithful dragomen who did their best to save us from being swindled in the bazaars. In the days of his successor, their vocabulary was limited to "Yok" and "Yassak"—"no" and "forbidden."

Beneath the surface of life in Turkey there was always a grim undercurrent of cruelty. And in that land there is more unnecessary human suffering than in any land of the world. There were dens in the town of Angora where Christian deserters—Conchies, perhaps—were kept, sometimes in chains. We used to see them marching out between their guards to work on the railway. Thin, grey, starved creatures, dying on their feet. Later on our men suffered in exactly the same way and about four-fifths of them died.

When the men went to Changri we kept our orderlies, and throughout captivity our orderlies were safe. But the rest of the men worked on the roads and railways all over Turkey, hundreds of miles from their officers, and the greater part of them died.

For the first two or three weeks of this season of exploration we lived in a Greek hotel at the bottom of the town. As hotels go in that part of the world, it was a good one. Downstairs there was the public eating-room on one side of the entrance and the coffee-room on the other; and upstairs there was a landing with a settee and a few chairs, and nine bedrooms. The beds were quite comfortable, but were infested with vermin, and the smell from the drain was perfectly awful. This was not the whole of the premises, for it formed one side only of a hollow square. The other three sides were occupied by Turkish soldiers, and the hollow square was really a caravanserai. Those rooms which faced the rear, into the hollow square, were the most infested, but the smell was the same everywhere. There was no garden, but a narrow space, cut off from the road by palings, was planted with half a dozen small trees, and used as an outdoor café.

The whole fifteen of us, from the Wank and from the Agricultural College, were established here. A certain number of sentries were at our disposal for explorations, shopping, etc., but we were not allowed to go out alone except within the palings, and there was a guard on the gate. We took our meals in the public room downstairs, together with the general public who patronized the hotel, Turkish officers for the most part. There were plenty of things to eat, not bad either when once one had got used to their greasy way of cooking, and they were cheap. But even so they were for the most part beyond our slender means, and it became quite a work of art to select so wisely as to fill one's stomach without emptying one's purse. All we had was paid for in cash at the time, and there were so many clamant uses for cash. Clothes, for example. An Armenian tailor came and measured us for suits, and used to come and try them on. He was a Roman Catholic and it was from him that we first learned that the Roman Catholic Armenians had been spared. He spoke a little French, and while trying on our clothes he used to whisper tales of the horrors of the preceding months. All the town was whispering them, all, that is to say, who were not Turkish. And they whispered in the greatest fear and trembling. Even Turks sometimes referred to the murders, and even they were impressed by slaughter upon so grand a scale; for it was the murder of a nation. It was as though

England had tried to destroy the whole of the Welsh race, and was still whispering about the deed. I remember one day we visited what had been the headquarters of the merchants of tiftik, the hair of the Angora goat. It was battered about and locked up, for with the death of the Armenian traders the tiftik trade had died. The Turkish guard who accompanied us grinned and drew his hand across his throat. Armenian refugees from Constantinople were interned in Angora. For the most part they were professional men, and they were all Russian subjects. They appeared to have no occupation, except to play backgammon all day long in a café they frequented. Most of them spoke French and a few English, and they, too, whispered sometimes as we sat near and sipped our coffee. Greeks whispered of the massacres, they did not know if their turn would come next. I remember a laborious conversation two of us held with a Greek boy, by the aid of a Turkish vocabulary. He had seen much that took place in Angora.

It seems, in writing this account, as though the greater part of our time was spent out of doors; but this was not really the case. For a few hours a day we got out, and we made the most of it, but for very many weary hours a day we were shut in. We had no books except a few French plays lent to us by a Turkish officer; one was "La Foi," by Brieux, and I occupied myself by translating it into English. We had chess, and that was all. When it was warm enough we used to sit in the chairs outside and watch the passers-by, and in the evenings we sat in the common room upstairs and talked. On the whole, we got on pretty well together, though things got very strained one evening when we had a thought-reading *séance*. It really must have been exceedingly annoying for the true believers to find that the whole affair was faked. I know I got behind a naval man in a corner and laughed until I nearly burst, but dared not let my face be seen. Things were so electric just then that a laugh might have brought about a thunderstorm. Especially when one of the most ardent spirits made the rest of us a perfectly solemn and heartfelt speech, beginning with "Gentlemen" and ending with a hope that our hearts were sufficiently pure to let in the light that would be vouchsafed us. Our hearts were not pure at all, but our merriment was. We got a manifestation of sorts, well thought out beforehand. But there was a lot of heartburning about ill-timed levity.

There was a certain amount of illness among us, from time to time. The officer with the pink drawers was really quite bad for a long time, and the remaining French officer nearly died, killed by kindness. That is before we had discovered that it was fatal to call in a Turkish doctor. As a rule, a Turkish doctor's one anxiety is to get you off to hospital where he may make money on your keep, and steal your boots. And from a Turkish hospital all escape is miraculous, all recovery is marvellous. If you were to go into a Turkish hospital with a broken leg the odds are that you would die of typhus. But we did not know that then. Our French friend was ill, so we sent for a doctor. Three came, at intervals during the day. The first was a captain, and he gave the patient a purgative of the right size for captains to give. The second was a major, and, as was only fit, he gave a much larger purgative, of the size that majors give. The third was a colonel, and whether his mission was to finish the job his subordinates had begun I do not know, but he strove manfully, and gave a similar dose of the size proper to colonels. That evening the Frenchman collapsed. He fainted and was carried off to bed by our stalwart Bill, the medical student of the party, a splendid person who was better than all the Turkish doctors in the world rolled in one. Much do we all owe to Bill, and none more than I do, for he nursed me through several bad illnesses; although, as he frankly stated on one occasion when I had paratyphoid, he hadn't "done fevers." A real wonder was our Bill, and I hope he will read this some day. From about that time until about a year later, when the doctors from Kut-el-Amara joined up with us at Afion, Bill was the camp physician-in-chief, and were I ill now I would as soon go to Bill as to anyone. He was a born healer. French was not his forte, but in the chemists' shops he always got what he wanted: went on until he did, or turned out on the counter the whole of the proprietor's stock. "Avez-vous ammoniated tincture of quinine?" he would ask. And if the man said "No," then Bill would counter with, "Avez-vous aucun else that will do similaire?" And in the end he would get it. As a linguist he had a natural perception of which words could be left out, or put in in English, without destroying the sense.

Two events happened to me about this time which were landmarks in that desert of dullness. It was in the Greek hotel that I received my first letter from home. A very great day indeed. And it was soon afterwards, in late November, that I spoke for the first time in Asia Minor to a woman. She was an old Roumanian in a cake-shop, and to her I said, "Bu kach para," being Turkish, my Turkish at least, for "What is the price of this?" I commend this sentence to the notice of those about to visit Turkey. It is one of the few worth knowing. It may seem strange that this should be noted as a landmark, but as a matter of fact I only spoke seven words to women between the 9th of August, 1915, and the 10th of September, 1918, and these were three of the seven. It is no small part of the multitude of causes that make prisoners queer, this deprivation of women's society. Men sink back into barbarism very rapidly when unbuoyed by the influence of women. They do not want the feminist, the creature doomed to the sterile affection of a little lamp-post-loving dog dragging at a lead. But they want to be helped by talking to mothers, lest they forget that motherhood is by far and away the greatest thing on earth.

At the beginning of November we moved into our house, up in the town, against the city wall. But a few days before that happened three more officers arrived from Constantinople. They were not newly captured. One had been taken on the same day as Bill, at Suvla Bay, and the other two were the oldest British prisoners of war in Turkey. I specify British, because we learned later on that there were Russian naval officers taken before war was officially declared, and prisoners of war because there were civil prisoners of earlier date. These two were members of the Egyptian police who had been given commissions in the army and sent out to test the disposition of the Arabs in that territory shown upon Old Testament maps as inhabited by the Philistines. The Arabs had turned upon them and handed them over to the Turks, and the ten or eleven months which elapsed before they joined us had been most eventful. I will not anticipate their story, for I do not know whether they will ever write it, further than to say that whereas we had seen the Armenian women and children setting forth on their fatal pilgrimage, these had seen it near its end. Their tale was truly ghastly. But there is one thing about one of them that I must write. He was an Egyptian, and by upbringing a Mohammedan, his name was Selim Zaki Kénâwi (he will forgive me if it is spelt wrongly). From the very start the Turks had tried their utmost to seduce him from his loyalty, and from the first to the last he had openly defied them. He was the most ardently loyal British person I have ever known. His plan was simply for Great Britain to own the whole earth and run it justly. I forget how many times he had been court-martialled on the charge of being a rebel, but it was several. They had tried the religious business too, and a venerable personage whom Zaki irreverently termed "a holy bloody religious man" had taken off his turban and solemnly asked, "Will you fight against this, Zaki Effendi?" But Zaki stood fast, and became more British than ever. It took some doing in his position, but he had the guts of a man. After he had been a couple of months with us he was sent for to Constantinople and again tested, both by intimidation and bribery. Enver Pasha, the Commander-in-Chief of the Turkish Army, the adventurer, the murderer, both privately and wholesale, the biggest scoundrel unhanged—I regret he is still unhanged—even himself sent for Zaki and offered him a choice between death and a commission in the Turkish Army. But Zaki never even thought which to choose. He chose death. But he did not die, although they sent him in the winter on the awful march to Sivas in its frozen mountains to be imprisoned among the Russians. There was typhus raging there, and there was more than a chance that his throat would be cut by the way. But he came safely through, and eventually rejoined us at Afion. An Egyptian tested as was Zaki should have a fine future in his own land.

The third new arrival, he from Suvla Bay, had suffered a curious adventure. In an attack he had been shot, and when he came to it was to find himself built into a temporary rampart of corpses. He was one of the corpses, and a Turk, with his rifle resting across his head, was firing away at our trench. He flapped about a bit, and was so fortunate as to become one of the seventeen officers who were kept as samples on Gallipoli.

I do not propose to give many personal histories, but without a few it would not be easy to convey to others what a strange selection from fate's claws we earlier pre-Kut prisoners were. Until Kut brought up our numbers to a large figure, every one of us, officer or man, was the survivor, perhaps the sole survivor, of some great adventure. Such as one I will refer to as the Squire: the day he was captured at Suvla Bay one hundred and two officers were "missing" on Gallipoli, and he alone came through. Such as Chok, our gigantic Yorkshireman, who, after braining a Turk with an axe, being blown up by a shell, and seeing his regiment almost wiped out, came through alone to us suffering from what is now known as shell-shock. Such as Dinkie, disabled by a bullet through the foot, who had to sham death while bayoneted ever so many times, and who had fortitude enough to sham it long enough. Such as Bill, who was shot through the neck; and who, long before he was well, was cast with other sick and wounded into a den in Constantinople, where he spent whole days wrestling single-handed with wounds and disease. This was the place where Enver visited the prisoners, and smiled and said it was good enough for the British. Very many died. Very many were saved by Bill.

CHAPTER VI

THE FIRST WINTER

IT was in the first week of November that we moved into the house allotted to us in the town. It was in a good quarter, about half-way up the hill, and it was a very good house as houses go in Asia Minor. In front there was a narrow street, and the building opposite to us was popularly supposed to be the Angora University. It was, at any rate, a school of large boys or small men; and I think we must have looked right into the University Museum, for there was a mouldy-looking stuffed owl there. On our left was another large house, at first used as a military hospital; but, when all the patients had died, restored to its purpose of a boys' school, small boys who used to make cutthroat signs to us. Our right flank rested upon a dunghill, or, rather, a kitchen midden, a public store of all manner of beastliness and the playground of the little schoolboys. Behind us was a dark, damp, narrow passage, beloved of dead cats, bounded on the one side by the school and our house, and on the other by the city wall. The hill was so steep that the entrance from the passage was two stories higher up than the main entrance from the street. We used the back door, for the main entrance was nailed up. The two bottom stories were uninhabitable, and by us unused. They contained stables and store-rooms. In the floor of one of the rooms there was a well, and beneath the floor there was the usual cess-pit. The next floor was on a level with our entrance, and contained a small kitchen and four bedrooms, one of which Derrick and I shared. The floor above that contained another kitchen, three bedrooms, and a large hall we used as a mess-room. Above that again was a small room containing a jumble of more or less useless articles, a sort of lumber-room, in fact, and a great many cubby-holes and recesses in the walls and under the roof. Above that again was an unwalled, roofed space used for hanging clothes to dry.

The house was owned by an Armenian woman who had found some means of adapting herself to terrible circumstances, and of conciliating the Turks. There were a number of such forlorn women in the town, and I, for one, do not blame them.

To this lady, who lived further down the street, we paid rent. So the Turkish Government was actually providing us with nothing at all except our four shillings a day. For we rented the house furnished, very little furnished.

The first fortnight of our stay here I passed in bed with persistent fever.

We had not long been in residence when some more prisoners turned up; the officers of a second submarine, and two or three others. They stayed for a while in the hotel, and then we divided forces and made two houses of it. Our house was already rather overcrowded, and it was impossible to take in half a dozen more.

The new house was a couple of hundred yards away from the old one, and was rented from a Turkish cavalry officer who kept a small bootshop in the town.

There was great friction over the division, but the less friction is emphasised the better. It is inevitable among prisoners.

Early in December Chukri Bey left Angora to go as Military Attaché to Berlin. We never met his like again. Swiftly and surely our privileges were stripped from us, and about the middle of December we were locked up for good and all. For the rest of our time in Angora we had no more walks, and our outings were cut down to one half-day a week for shopping. We were not even allowed to walk in the narrow passage behind the house for several weeks, though we did later regain that dismal right. It became exceedingly cold. Snow fell, and the temperature was often near zero. But we were too poor to spend much on fuel. Larger bills for our keep while in Constantinople came in, and their amount was deducted from our pay. We had to try to buy blankets and underclothes. And we had to store fuel for the kitchen fire. Gold had disappeared now from circulation, and silver was fast disappearing also. The Turkish Government used to pay us in paper, and as they had not yet struck small notes, they paid us in fivers in bulk, and left us to settle among ourselves how to change them. It was often almost impossible to do so in the bazaar, and our mess secretary and the shopping orderly had a very trying time.

In that house we could not afford to have charcoal braziers in our rooms, as is the custom in Turkey and as we did later at Afion. The kitchen fire had to be kept from failing, but the kitchen was far too small to sit in, it would hold two people standing up. We had a stove in the mess-room, and we used to light it about tea-time every afternoon. For the rest of the day, if the sun shone, we used to congregate in the two front rooms which got a narrow band of sunshine, until the roof warmed up, and then we used to sit on the tiles. It was warmer on the tiles than indoors, so long as there was no wind, even though the shady slope of the roof were thick with snow. When it snowed, or was windy, or rained, or was clouded over it was warmer indoors, warmest in bed.

Entire lack of exercise is bad for Britons, and looking back to that winter I marvel that we quarrelled so little. Once the split of houses was over we practically did not disagree at all. We played cards, and chess, and backgammon. We had a few books. We talked. And we were silent. Sometimes we had concerts. We were not much in the singing line, but we made plenty of noise. Also there were alleviations. Those must not be left out, or this chapter would seem more gloomy than is true. A few parcels came, a few home letters, some food, and some books. Several of us accomplished the reading of Gibbon's "Decline and Fall," which probably we should never have done except in prison. And extraordinarily interesting we found it, especially the later volumes which deal with the history of the Crusades and the Turks. And I had two occupations unshared by the rest, which took up much time, for I wrote verses and had jaundice.

There was a sheet of ice on the floor, where water had been spilled, when I went to bed, and twelve days later, when I got up, there was the same ice still there. So cold it was. It was too cold to hold a book, so I used to lie all day and devise meetings and dinners with my most loved friends after the war.

From the tiles we had a widespread view of snow-covered plain and range beyond range of mountains. The ground floor, so to speak, of Asia Minor is about 3,000 feet above sea level. That is the average elevation of the plains, and from that level rise the mountains. They are bare and bleak, unclothed by woods, white in the winter, green for a brief and beautiful spring, and for the rest of the year the colour of dust. Even in the tropics I have not seen more gorgeous sunsets than those we used to watch from the roof top, while below us lay the dark streets of the town, channeled through the white roofs, and half-obscured by a mist of smoke.

In the daytime those roofs were not altogether without interest. Sometimes we saw people on them, but more often cats; real Angora long-haired cats, basking, fighting, and love making. We got to know a lot of them by sight.

The street, too, was sometimes blocked by camels; sometimes fierce-looking, armed ruffians strode along it; and there were a few pretty girls who had a kind eye for the prisoners. And while the house on our left was still a hospital, the town band used to come two or three times a week and play excruciating music. But that can hardly be ranked as an alleviation! The University, too, was a source of joy to us, thoroughly pharisaical joy that we were not as they. For they were a slimy crowd of undersized semi-demi-educated creatures not to be compared with the stalwart murderers of the tanneries down below in the gorge. They loved processions and patriotic demonstrations. I remember once they carried out in procession a huge lath and paper ship meant to celebrate some Turkish naval victory: it was about the time that the "Hilal" newspaper announced that the Turkish navy still consisted of over 300 units which floated. They must have included life-buoys.

All through that winter the news was bad for us, heartening for the Turks. Russia was driven back. Bulgaria came in against us. We evacuated the peninsula of Gallipoli, and a spirited, but wholly imaginary, account appeared in the "Hilal" describing how our rearguard fought and was destroyed to the last man. And Turkey began to dream and talk of an overwhelming force concentrating for an attack on the Suez Canal. The patriotic Zaki laughed at the idea of Egyptians submitting to be "liberated" by Turkey. And we were all pretty optimistic despite the gloomy news. "You are optimistic because you are prisoners," said the French-speaking and wholly abominable officer who at this time had charge of us. And though he knew it not, he spoke a great truth. For prisoners are the most optimistic people in the world. For one thing, they dare not be otherwise; but the chief reason is one analogous to the action of vaccination or inoculation. For in the minds of prisoners anti-bodies to the disease of pessimism multiply so fast that their combative antitoxin keeps pace with the worst of news. This was most noticeable throughout captivity, and, like Livingstone's famous insensitiveness in the grip of the lion, it was a cheery feature of an otherwise unpleasant experience.

This officer was of the East Eastern, dyed as to the skin only by a smear of the West. Once he had been as far West as Sophia, and on that, fortified by pornographic French literature, he based his claim to civilisation. When I was ill with paratyphoid, and partially delirious, he used to visit me while the rest were upstairs at lunch, and used to try to poison my mind with his views on the downfall of England. But the skipper, our senior officer, took this in hand, locked me in and him out, and utterly refused him permission to visit me. He used also to be as uncivil as he dared to Zaki, who longed to cut his throat; but this Turk was not a man who dared much, and he was shut up in that direction also. He used to drop in to tea, and call us "mon cher." He *was* an unlikeable creature. But after Christmas he cooled off, for the reason that we made him drunk and foolish. This is not the tale of a select seminary, but of full-blooded, hard-hearted prisoners of war, who had not much joy in their lives. So I shall describe Christmas, and pray for the mercy of the court. To be judged by our peers we should be judged by soldier and sailor prisoners.

We had been locked up just long enough to hate it by Christmas, and we determined to have as merry an evening as we could. We were helped in this in several ways. First by ourselves, for we succeeded in buying some rum in the town. Secondly, by the American Ambassador, may his name be praised, who sent us a real generous Christmas hamper, with a ham, whisky, rum, port, cigars, and chocolate. A gorgeous individual, all gold and scarlet, came all the way from Constantinople to bring it. And, thirdly, by the Turks: for they gave us leave to congregate for the one evening all together in the other house, and they provided twelve Christmas trees! There were no woods nearer than two and a half days' journey distant, and yet they sent out a party of soldiers who brought in twelve small fir trees. I think they were a little apologetic that there were not enough trees to go round; and we regretted it, too, for firewood was scarce. But it was a kindly thought, and they deserve all credit for it. I had not had a Christmas tree of my own for about twenty-five years.

There was rivalry between the two houses, just as there is at school, just as there was rivalry between the two separate camps at Afion two years later. But we sank it for the feast, and pooled all our resources. Before dinner we sat round braziers and absorbed much alcohol: very much: so much that one officer missed his dinner, although we shouted in his ear that the war was over. Even that he could not hear. Even the word "Peace" failed to rouse him. But he came round later, and ate a huge dinner all by himself. We had turkey, and ham, and plum-pudding, real American Embassy plum-pudding. We had also whisky. We had cigars, and port, and again whisky. Then the evening began in earnest, near the stove, all as near as possible to a wash basin full of hot rum punch. We had a concert in full swing, when the Army Corps Commander, the Commandant of Angora, the officer in charge of the prisoners, and an interpreter came in. On a chair, with his back to the door, stood the cook, and he was a noted songster who sang principally one song. I shall have to paraphrase the only line I propose to quote, but it does not lose any of its sense if reproduced as:

"Little pigs lie with their backs all bare, umph bare," etc.

The Army Corps Commander was a dignified person. He was the swine who had locked us up. But except in his own person he loathed swine as a true Mohammedan should. All mention of the pig family, or of those good things, ham and bacon, were anathema to him. The Commandant of the Place was likewise a person of very great dignity. Some effort was made to stop the song, for these people had come on a state visit; to see their Christmas trees, perhaps. But the Army Corps Commander waved all interference aside with a superb gesture of benignity. "Let the song of welcome proceed," he said, and these four unwanted visitors sat down in a solemn row while the song did proceed, with pigs and pantomime in every verse. Prison life in Turkey was not without occasional gleams of merriment.

What the interpreter thought I don't know. He was an Armenian who had embraced Islam to save his skin, and he did not matter anyhow. The grandees did not wait long. We hoped to be able to "tank them up," for very nearly all Turkish officers drink pretty heavily, despite Islam. But they were too cautious. They and the interpreter departed. But our officer remained, and he was our reward. Him we rendered completely tight. So tight that at the end he stood upon a table and sang "God save the King" in English; though, up to then, he had always denied all knowledge of English. Zaki still wanted to cut his throat, and was with difficulty restrained.

Thus passed the Christmas of 1915; and it was just as well we did not know that two more Christmases would have to pass in the same way. We all walked home to our house unaided. But the officer in charge of us slackened off his unwelcome camouflage friendship from that day, for he knew what a fool he had been.

January was very cold, and we were pleased to learn, towards the end of it, that we were all to be moved to Afion-Kara-Hissar, where the other British officers were interned. We were thoroughly sick of Angora, and of being locked up. No change was to be expected under the present Army Corps Commander, who hated us as much as we hated him. And really I don't blame him very much looking back upon it in cold blood. British prisoners are perfect brutes to manage. If they are allowed to run things themselves, they run them very well indeed, but they also run away. If they are given much liberty they walk about as if they own the place. Not out of pride or display, but just because they actually feel as if they owned it. I felt, we each felt, as though we British owned Angora. They will never, no not ever, not even if they die, feel, or seem to feel, or pretend to feel that their captors are as good men as they, let alone that they are better. Again and again we received instructions—even now I can hardly admit ever receiving "orders" of such a kind, hence "instructions"—to salute all Turkish officers whom we met in the streets. And each time those instructions were ignored. We saluted senior officers, not those of rank equivalent to our own. If, on the other hand, British prisoners are given no liberty, they continually struggle for more, and make the lives of the Turks a burthen to them. A Turkish officer of any grade always prefers to get one of a lower grade to do his work, and to attend to his interviews for him. We never acquiesced in this for one moment. If possible we raided the senior officer's privacy. If that was not possible, we sent his junior to fetch him. And if that failed we ruined his peace of mind by continually writing letters to him. When any outside person of importance visited us we complained bitterly of all we resented, and were not afraid. Turks don't understand that attitude at all. Their method is to give strict orders, to have those orders obeyed in semblance, and disobeyed in private, until, in the course of time the orders lapse and become obsolete. Then the senior officer awakes from his pleasant slumber, makes a lot of new orders, and goes to sleep again. In no circumstance will he remain awake, give reasonable orders, and see to it himself that they are reasonably carried out. It is difficult for the Turk to keep his mind, his will, or whatever you like to call it, firmly and steadily opposed to the wills of others, whether prisoners, or his subordinates, or subject peoples. He simply cannot do it. His method is to be unreasonably lax for a long time, and then unreasonably severe for a short time, so that the resultant line of progression may be more or less straight. Thus, diagramatically expressed, these two lines, T for Turkish and B for British, point in the same direction, but are quite different in kind:

T. etc.

B. etc.

It follows that in Turkey there are no standing orders. None, that is to say, that live long. There are files, rooms, whole houses full of dead ones. But can you call orders "standing" when they do not stand?

In a small way, this conflict between ideas of government made life troublesome for us in Turkey, and even more troublesome for the Turks. But we were a small matter. If the main facts of their history were similarly plotted as a diagram, it would be found very like my line T.: and the result is the ruination of one of the most fruitful lands on the face of the earth; the production of nothing, save only cruelty and unnaturally debased races; and the present-day collapse and disintegration of the Ottoman Empire.

Although we expected to hear at any moment that we were to pack up and go to Afion, the date of our departure continued to recede. We really had some things to pack now. It is extraordinary how quickly things accumulate, even in prison. We were all anxious to go, especially the skipper, who thought Afion would not be so difficult to escape from. He was always thinking of escape, and at last did get clear away, but not until the latter half of 1918. The account of that truly great and successful adventure has been written in *Blackwood's Magazine.*

Personally I had given up the idea; my continual bad health had forced me to abandon all hope of escape.

In Turkey all moves happen as did our move to Afion. You are told that you will go, and nothing happens. Having been lied to consistently on all possible occasions, after a time you conclude that this is just one more lie. Then, quite suddenly, you are told that you are to go now at once. Hastily you pack up, sell off what you can, take what you can of the rest with you, and go. At the other end you find that nobody expects you at all. Either they have never been informed that you are coming; or they have been informed of it so long ago that they have forgotten; or, most likely of all, they, too, have thought it was just one more lie.

How the dickens this people ever managed to run an empire is a holy mystery to me. I don't believe they did. I believe that all real organisation, such as it was, has been done by Greeks, Armenians and Jews, by subject people, slaves, half-breeds and poly-breeds.

They put up a wonderful fight in this war, despite the dearth of roads and railways. But they were staffed by Germans, and nobody denies that Germans can organize. But how the Turks hated them! With German organization the Turkish infantry can do very well indeed. They are tough and hardy to a degree hard to conceive. They can live on nothing and march all day. And they are brave. Poor devils, they need be. They are operated upon without anæsthetics, which were only kept for officers. They are half-starved, and they are mercilessly flogged and bastinadoed. I have seen recruits coming in chained in gangs; and I have seen the sick and wounded crawl with grey, leaden faces up from Angora station to the rough accommodation provided for them in the town. I have seen them leave their hospitals, too, generally in corpse-carts. If all else fails to kill them, typhus does not fail. As practically all Turks of the lower orders are lousy from birth to death, typhus rages among them. Lice give them typhus, bugs convey relapsing fever, and fleas the plague. Turks abound in all these insects. They may be said to be their natural fauna. But the toughness of the peasants causes them to survive as a race in spite of disease, in spite of ill-treatment, and in spite of continuous war.

At last, late at night on the 13th of February, 1916, we left Angora by train for Afion-Kara-Hissar. And to the station there came, to bid good-bye to us, the most mysterious person in Angora: so mysterious that I dare not mention him for fear, if he is still there, it might bring him into peril.

CHAPTER VII

AFION-KARA-HISSAR

AFTER about twenty-four hours in the train, a train that stopped at every station, I looked out into the night and saw a strange place where huge rocks rose up against the sky. The train was slowing down while I looked, and I thought to myself that it would be an interesting place to see by daylight. Afterwards I saw it by daylight: by the light of nine hundred and thirty-eight days and by the moonlight of many nights, and it no longer seemed so interesting. It was like the old legend where the fortunate man is given three wishes and each recoils upon his head. For this was Afion-Kara-Hissar.

Afion-Kara-Hissar means Opium Black Fort. Miles of white opium poppies are grown in the fields about the town, and the black fort—the Kara-Hissar—is a huge solitary rock rising up out of the town as out of a sea. The great plain, which stretches away for miles in every direction except the south, must have been an inland sea once, though it is now more than 3,000 feet above the level of the Mediterranean.

The Kara-Hissar is precipitous on all sides, hung round by cliffs, and there are few places where it can be climbed. The walls of an old fort grin along its rim like broken teeth; and there is a tradition that it was once besieged in vain for many years. In the days before gunpowder, provided that food and water did not fail and the garrison was faithful, it is hard to see how it could ever fall. We used to argue about its height, without result, but it cannot have been less than 600 feet from the town to the coronet of walls.

Afion is a natural junction among the highways of the mountains. The plain is ringed by the hills, and the passes through them lead to Afion. Xenophon crossed the plain, and Alexander the Great. The first crusade streamed past the mighty rock. And at the present day the Smyrna line joins on at Afion with the Constantinople—Bagdad railway. During the war all troops from Constantinople or Smyrna proceeding to either the Mesopotamian or Palestine fronts passed through Afion. And we watched them. The only aeroplane I saw during my captivity, flown by a German officer from Constantinople to Jerusalem, passed through Afion. And tens of thousands of storks on their annual migration passed by the same way in vast flocks.

It was an interesting place, true enough. But when is captivity interesting? After we had been there a year and a half we found that it had another title to fame, for we read in a book that it possessed perhaps the best known mosque of Dervishes in Turkey. The Dervishes we knew well enough by sight, with their long robes and high felt hats, like elongated brimless toppers. And we knew the mosque, too. It was well built; but it was modern and did not somehow look famous. Well, if the place was famous before, it is infamous all right now.

We arrived at about ten o'clock on a cold night and found that no one expected us. At any rate, they had made no preparations for our disposal. After some delay we were marched up from the station, about a mile, through the town, and ushered into a house that would have been better if it had been empty. For it had been used as a hospital, and had never been cleaned since. There were filthy bandages and other oddments about the floors. As usual, it was an Armenian house; for, although the Armenians of Afion were not actually massacred in or near the town, as at Angora, they had nearly all been deported at the time of the great Armenian drive. It was really a very good house, about the best I was ever in in Turkey, except at the end, in Smyrna. But except for the dirt of the hospital *débris* it was utterly bare.

When we woke up next morning we found we were quarantined on account of the typhus at Angora, as well as locked up in the ordinary way. But soon a cheery-looking Englishman with a pointed beard marched up the road outside and hailed us through the windows. This was a naval officer, the senior officer among the British prisoners at Afion, and from him we learned that much more freedom was to be expected here than we had known for a long while.

I forget how long our quarantine lasted, not more than a day or two, and then we were free to go out, accompanied by guards, to visit the other prisoners. There was one house, just on the opposite side of the Kara-Hissar, with, I think, nine French officers in it; and four or five hundred yards further on there was another house with nine or ten British officers, mostly naval, and about the same number of Russians. Of the Russians, four or five belonged to the Imperial Navy, and the rest were Merchant Service men, not really prisoners of war. In the Medrisseh, the large old Mohammedan school in the town, there were a lot more Russian merchant sailor officers and engineers. These Russians beat us all in duration of captivity, for they had all been seized before war actually was declared.

The French-Anglo-Russian community had the very great privilege of permanent permission, by daylight, to use a generous slice of rocky hill-side as a playground, and the Anglo-Russian house had a large garden in addition. They kept turkeys and chickens, and seemed to us to be extraordinarily fortunate people. And we shared their good luck to a large extent, for, though we had not the hill-side always at hand, we were allowed to come over with a guard every afternoon.

A few days after our arrival at Afion the three original naval officers of Angora moved from our rather crowded quarters into the French house. The skipper had marked it down as a good place to escape from, and in two of the naval officers of the Anglo-Russian house he had found men as daring as himself.

For five or six weeks things went smoothly. A good many parcels arrived, and letters from home, which mean so much. Altogether, captivity was as tolerable as could be expected. Spring was early that year, and snow fell only once after we had settled in. I embarked upon an awful career of writing verses, a regular orgie of production, and it took me so far from Turkey that at times it was hard to realize which was my real life, that in the Armenian house, or the wider one among the forests of Ceylon, where I wandered far and free. Buds were shooting, the sap began to sting in the veins of the trees, and in the caves the starlings built their nests. Spring is a season of charm wherever one may be, but in Turkey even that paradise contains a serpent, for the season of awakening rouses the things that bite from their winter sleep, and lying awake at night one can hear the prisoners stir and scratch themselves.

We had arrived at Afion so completely penniless that the Turkish Commandant, at our request, sent a wire to the American Ambassador asking for money. The Ambassador rose to the occasion and sent up £Tq.3 a head. Prices had already begun the giddy climb I have already indicated, and our Turkish pay was already hardly enough to keep body and soul together. The three pounds became a monthly grant, later it was increased to five, and before we left Turkey it had become eighteen. Let no one think that on this we were rich. But it was a great thing to feel that our plight was not forgotten.

Some of the adventures that had landed prisoners at Angora have been briefly described. Let me give a few of those that had brought others to Afion. The first I must mention is that of an Australian observer, for it tells of a very gallant deed performed by one of our enemies, and even the bitterness of war should not be allowed to obscure glorious deeds. In December one of our aeroplanes crashed into the sea about a mile, more or less, from the coast of the Gallipoli peninsula held by the Turks. The pilot sank, but the observer was buoyed up by his life-saving waistcoat until he lost consciousness in the bitterly cold water. When he came to his senses again he found himself ashore, a prisoner, and he was told that a German officer had swum out and brought him in: swum out into that December sea to save an enemy. Let that stand to the credit of Germany, and the other story I shall tell to the discredit of Turkey. It is the tale of Joe, a sturdy Yorkshire sailor man, a naval reserve officer, who was sent into a bay on the southern coast of Anatolia in command of a boat. They hoped to locate a submarine base, but they were ambushed instead. Joe was hit in the neck by a great lump of a Snyder bullet, which had first passed through the side of the boat. The survivors were captured, and Joe, who rode as a sailor, travelled many painful miles on horseback. He was operated on in the most primitive fashion, by being held down by soldiers while a Turkish doctor lugged the bullet by main force from its lodging place at the base of his jaw. Finally he reached the civilised town of Smyrna, and was there confined in the local war office, a large building facing one of the main streets. Just below his window was the window of the office used by the Commandant of the place. For three days and nights Joe was not allowed out of that room for any purpose whatsoever. There was no convenience of any sort in the room, but all his demands to be allowed out, even for five minutes, were met by a fixed bayonet. Still, there was the window, and Joe was a clean person. Eventually the high and mighty person in the room below complained, and his complaint brought Joe's sufferings to an end. It is disgusting to write of these things, but captivity among a disgusting people is a disgusting fact. Why should white books and blue books have the monopoly?

In the last week of March we had exciting news. The skipper and two other naval officers had gone. They simply got out of their windows at night, rendezvoused on the hill-side, and struck for the coast. They had made ample preparation in the way of training, and they carried enough food to last them for two weeks. The skipper was in the French house, and he had not told them his plan, so they were taken by complete surprise. But they rose to the occasion like men, and showed the greatest skill in leading the Turks gently away from the scent. We all thought them jolly good sportsmen. So successfully was the escape concealed, and so lax were the guards, that it was four days before the Turks discovered that they were three prisoners short. Even then they could not believe it. They looked in the beds and under them, and called plaintively in odd corners, hoping the whole thing was a joke. It was only the letter to the Commandant which had been left behind that finally convinced them. Then there was the devil to pay.

In Turkey it was not the guards that kept the prisoners in, but the country. Guards there were in plenty, but they were often lax and until this escape there were no regular roll calls. But the country is a terrifically hard place to get out of. To begin with, it is no easy matter to find one's way through mountains with only a small-scale map. I doubt if the country has ever been properly surveyed. Then there is the language difficulty and the cutthroat character of the inhabitants. Water, too, is scarce, and food unobtainable. And the size of the country is vastly greater than most people seem to imagine. Asia Minor is roughly 600 miles long and 400 miles broad: a larger country than Spain. And it had no frontier which abutted upon friendly country nearer than the Caucasus, an almost hopeless journey to attempt. East there are the Taurus mountains, and beyond them desert, so that direction is out of the question. North, west, and south there is the sea. And our information was that very few boats were likely to be available. So that even when a party overcame the great difficulties of the land journey, and reached the coast, there was always a very strong probability of their having to give themselves up to get food.

Two days after this escape had taken place, and two days before the Turks discovered it, a new party of prisoners arrived in Afion. It was hard luck that they should have come at such a time, for they were very worn and required good treatment. There were a few men and about nine officers, all from the Mesopotamian front. They had been taken at different times, and had joined up on the way. It was always the prisoners from the Mesopotamian front who had the worst time on the journey. For, in those days, the Bagdad railway stopped short hundreds of miles from the fighting line, and prisoners had to make the awful desert marches as best they could. Six of these had come down out of the sky, and two had been taken in a stranded barge during the retreat of the 6th Division to Kut-el-Amara. Each had his separate adventure and wonderful escape. In few places in the world can so varied a body of adventurers have been gathered as there were at Afion then. We had British, French, Russians, Ukrainians, Poles, Black Sea Greeks, Jews, and Russian Italians, besides all sorts of obscure Baltic and Eastern European people. The Roumanians and Serbs did not come until later. There were men who had dropped from the heavens, and men who had risen out from the depths of the sea; men from the Dardanelles, from Mesopotamia, from the Sinai Peninsula, and from the plain of Troy. Later on, we had additions from Persia, Palestine, and the Caucasus. Between us we had seen and wandered over most of Europe, Asia, Africa, America, and the Southern Seas; and we spoke most of the tongues of the earth, and some others. Had we combined, we might have written a pretty good guide book to the world; its hills and its heavens, its cities and its wide spaces; and we would have puzzled the builders of Babel.

To live among us was a liberal education, and some of us were boys who had hardly left school when war began. And the setting of this drama was a dingy, dirty Turkish town, with mud-coloured, flat-topped houses, and narrow, wretched streets.

The new-comers had nothing but what they stood up in. One, a short, stout man, had been stripped naked when he was captured, and had been led before the Turkish general dressed only in a sack given him in charity. Since that, however, he had succeeded in getting some clothes more suitable to his considerable dignity: "The Admiral," we used to call him: he was a member of the Royal Indian Marine. Several were unwell, and all were in need of good food and a rest. One of them used to tell a story of the attention received on the journey from a Turkish doctor; a story of the kind we grew to know as typically Turkish. This officer attended a Turkish hospital to have an ulcer in his leg dressed. The bandage seemed a bit more than secondhand, and the officer asked for a clean one. But the Turkish doctor refused, assuring him, in French, that it was *tout à fait stérilizé*, absolutely sterilized. So it was applied. But on the way home the officer felt it crawl, and, removing it, found that it contained nine lice. Is it any wonder that typhus was rife?

In so far as it was possible, we had to fit our new friends out, for, of course, the Turks gave them nothing but a bare Armenian house, which cost them nothing. What our captors would have done with us all if they had not prepared homes for us by slaying the Armenians it is hard to imagine. Probably they would not have been troubled to keep us at all. Those poor Armenians were our sacrifice.

We shared out whatever few articles of clothes, pipes, tobacco, and food we could spare, and the new-comers prepared to take a rest cure. But they were doomed to disappointment. The next two months were certainly the most trying I have ever spent in my life. When at last the Commandant did discover that three officers were missing, there was a tremendous uproar. The first thing that happened was that the Commandant, whose duty it was to safeguard the prisoners, telegraphed to Constantinople resigning his job, and stating that he had handed over to a vicious old gentleman, known as the Kolassi, who was second in command. He hoped in this way to land the Kolassi with the responsibility of the escape. But the Kolassi was not fool enough to take over short measure, and the Commandant was obliged to retain his command pending inquiry. Of course, we were all locked up, and inter-house communication completely prevented. The place bristled with bayonets. Then we were all ordered to pack up and be prepared to move in half-an-hour. The small Turkish naval officer who was bearing the brunt of his superior's wrath waxed almost tearful as he lectured the occupants of the French house on the sin of lying, and told them of the awful punishments of hell. All sorts of intrigues went on among the Turks, and the blame of the escape was shuffled round like the game of Old Maid. No one had the very slightest idea when they had gone, where they had gone, or how they had gone. I doubt if they know to this day how long a start they had. The Commandant, in his wriggles to avoid punishment, did a most dastardly thing, a typically Turkish thing: for he reported officially that the officers who had escaped had been on parole and had broken it. This was a downright lie. One of the fugitives had been senior British officer in the camp, and the Commandant had asked him to give a parole for the whole lot of us; but he had immediately and unhesitatingly refused to do anything of the kind. This lie was calculated to put the prisoners who had escaped in a very perilous position if recaptured, and I have no doubt at all that it affected the treatment meted out to the rest of us.

When we had hastily packed up we were mustered in a street in the desolate Armenian quarter. Not only the British, but all the other nationalities too, including a large number of Russian merchant sailor men whom we had never seen before. Here we were carefully counted, and were then marched away in the direction of the Kara-Hissar, the wise among us carrying everything we could. It is folly to be separated from one's baggage in Turkey.

Right under the Kara-Hissar, so close that a stone thrown strongly out from above might crash through its roof, was an Armenian church. A fairly large building of grey stone with iron-barred windows and an iron door. Outside the door was a very small courtyard paved with rough slabs of stone, and along one side of the church ran a stone-flagged pathway, flanked by a narrow strip of ground on which grew two pear trees and an acacia. Opposite to the church, on the other side of the tiny courtyard, was a tall white building which had been an Armenian school. This church was selected as our prison. It was the only place in the town which could have held us, except the Medrisseh.

As we approached the church, up a steep street and a flight of steps, we passed a number of unfortunate Armenian women and children who had been turned out to make room for us. They sat by the road with their little bundles, looking very miserable indeed, and I am sure we did not want to rob them of their refuge.

We all, officers and orderlies, marched into the church, and the iron door was closed. There were guards outside the door and inside the door, and guards on the flagged path without. At the western end of the church were two galleries, one above the other; one was given to our orderlies, and the other had an armed guard in it. There were over a hundred of us in the church, most of us with home-made beds, some with chairs, tables, basins, boxes, and cooking pots. The older prisoners had by this time made benches and mess tables and other pieces of furniture, and there were two dogs and a cat. By the time that carts had brought up the last of our things, the place was so full that one could hardly move. We kept a clear passage way down the centre, from the door to the altar, and the remainder of the space was thronged with all manner of men and all manner of objects precious to their owners. Four Russian naval officers were the luckiest, for they were given a vestry to themselves.

That night, while the French and British slept, patrols of Russians took it in turns to keep watch for the massacre they expected. Up and down the central aisle they marched, two at a time, until dawn showed that our heads were still on our shoulders. They knew the Turks better than we, but we loved our sleep.

CHAPTER VIII

THE ARMENIAN CHURCH

FOR the next two weeks we were not allowed out of the church at all, not even into the little courtyard. Three at a time we were escorted by sentries to the latrine beneath the school opposite, and that was the only momentary glimpse we had of the outer world, save what little could be seen through the barred windows. We were treated exactly as the Turks treat their criminals. And after a few days even that small crossing beneath the sky was denied us, for they built a new latrine, a most slipshod, amateur affair, up against the wall of the church, where there was a small door. Fortunately, the building was high in proportion to its floor space, and some of the windows were broken.

Typhus broke out among us, and two people died; one Russian, and one British orderly. But, by the grace of God, the plague stopped there, as though by magic. Fortunately, we were clean when we went in. But the very dust of the place grew septic, and small cuts and grazes grew into sores that were hard to heal.

The Commandant was superseded by a hard-faced man whose service had been chiefly in the wilds of Southern Arabia. This person's name was Maslûm Bey, and I watch the newspapers daily to see some notice that he has been hanged, but so far I have watched in vain. The charges against him are in the hands of the Government, and I trust his doom is sure. But of that later, if indeed it can be put into a book at all.

Roll call was now held daily, twice a day at first, and in the beginning it was, as it ought to be, very strict. Each person, as his name was called, had to walk up and be recognized. But later on, like all things Turkish, it lapsed into a matter of form, satisfied by an incoherent "Hullo!" and an arm waved from behind a crowd.

Each group of friends formed a mess, which had its table in some corner of the church, or on the altar platform; and on the floor beds were grouped in rows or square kraals, with their owners' belongings ranged close by. Order of a sort grew out of chaos. The orderlies were luckier than the officers, for they cooked against the wall of the church outside, and a certain number of them were allowed to go shopping so many days a week. For, as the Turks could not undertake to feed us, they had to permit our orderlies to go to the bazaar. These orderlies were really rather wonderful fellows. They managed to pick up enough kitchen Turkish to bargain with the shopkeepers; they knew the ruling rates of all principal articles of food; kept wonderful accounts, despite the dearth of change; chaffed their guards, and were very popular in the town. One could not but have the highest admiration for them. And our cooks, too, did marvels. Led by a French sailor, who in private life was a chef at the Jockey Club in Paris, they became quite expert in dishing up the tasteless stuffs that Turks live on. And, despite some perfectly appalling rows, they kept their heads and their tempers.

There never was such a pandemonium as that church! You can't lock up a lot of hot-blooded men and starve them of everything that living means without outbreaks of a sort. Not that there were many quarrels among officers: they were very rare indeed, but the noise, and uproar, and shouting, singing, and drinking until all hours of the early morning made the place like a thieves' kitchen in an old story-book. Hogarth could have painted it, but I don't know who could have described it. Certainly I can't. Except for a few hours before dawn, when there was a hush, the place was always full of noise. Drinking parties, gambling parties, singing parties, shouting parties: people learning languages, people arguing, people carpentering, and, in the midst of it all, people thinking out problems in silence, people reading, people writing. I used to sit on my bed and write verses all day long sometimes. Another officer wrote two plays while we were there, and, what is more, rehearsed and produced them. And in that place the Russians made great music. They are a wonderful people in that way. Where the Russians gather together, there you have a choir. And the place was full of musical instruments, violins, guitars, mandolines; played by masters, played by learners, and played by people who did not and never could learn.

The worst feature was the heavy drinking. A good many of us thought that the Turks would, in the circumstances, have been wise to forbid liquor. But they could not resist the chance of making money, and it flowed in. Beastly native spirit for the most part, and synthetic violet-flavoured Greek brandy: some good stuff, too, ordered from Constantinople, and paid for by cheque. "Let us eat and drink, for to-morrow we die," was the motto of that place. And, by Jove! we did. There were dinners and there were suppers, for many parcels had come in, and there were "blinds." People had birthdays; nation feasted nation; or nations feasted themselves. Less quiet than Niagara Falls was that place and nearly as wet. I regret much of this, but do not condemn it. Let no one judge the events of a time like that unless he or she is quite certain he knows what it was like in its entirety. There were men, keen, ardent, fighting men, in the prime of their age, robbed of everything that goes to ballast life. They were held back from that which they had set out to do, to fight for their country. The regulars knew that their whole career perhaps was ruined, that all the chances of the war were not for them, and that stagnation in their chosen profession was the price of their ill-fortune. The civilians who had donned uniform for the great adventure knew that their sacrifice had been in vain, and that there was no great adventure for them any more. The older men knew that their businesses were going to ruin, and the younger knew that they were missing the most important years of their training. All this made gunpowder of men's souls. And we were starved, not of bread, but of all else that life holds good. Starved of work, starved of amusement, starved of news of a world in the making, starved of the society of women, starved of freedom itself. I do not think that many outside people are fit to condemn the excesses of that place.

There was one man, not an Englishman, who slept all day. But if one awoke in the silent hour one could see him with a little lamp by his side, smoking pipe after pipe of opium. I think the other way was better than that.

It must be added that the French, as a body, behaved extraordinarily well. And with that I will change the subject.

Apart from the noise, the place was intensely irritating to live in. We were so very close to each other. It is unpleasant to be cooped up with too much of one's fellow man. The sweetest temper would revolt in time. And we were of such wide varieties as regards personal habits. It is the small habits that are sharp enough to prick. But, looking back at captivity, I have often felt horribly small-minded, and I daresay a lot of others have too.

After two weeks' complete confinement, one day the doors were opened, and we were made free of the tiny courtyard and the flagged path outside. When we were all out at once there was hardly room to turn round, but it was a very great improvement.

The yard, about ten yards square, was used for everything, from football to boxing. Someone had received a set of gloves in a parcel, and they were a godsend. There used to be some very pretty scraps in the mornings, and some very hefty slogging matches. Several of the better performers set up schools of pugilism. It was very good fun, but the filthy drain oozed in the courtyard, and the very dust was poisonous. Several officers got very sore eyes, and the only thing to do with a scratch was to dab it with iodine at once.

I remember George, a Russian Pole with a fiery nature, sitting on a stone by me one day and watching a ferocious but perfectly good-tempered round which drew much blood. He was intensely interested and thought it a noble sport—for Britishers. For, as he said frankly, if anyone were to hit him on the nose like that he would not feel his honour satisfied until he had exchanged shots with the aggressor. This shows what different angles of view different people in that church had.

Meanwhile, two things hung in the balance, and we hungered for news of both.

The three daring escapers had not yet been rounded up, and Kut was still besieged.

After eighteen days of marching through mountains, the three came within sight of the sea. But they were doomed to failure. They could not get down the precipitous gorge by which their guiding river plunged from the mountains, and they had not enough food to go back and round by another way. So they bought food from a shepherd, were given away, and recaptured. It was a sad end to a very brave attempt. Then the despicable meanness of the late Commandant's lie began to tell against them. They were treated as prisoners who had broken their word of honour, and cast into a filthy dungeon in Constantinople. There they awaited trial for over six months. Then they were court-martialled, and that, at any rate, should have been final. But it was far from it. The court found them guilty of attempting to escape, and gave them a not unjust sentence of two weeks' confinement. (I think the senior officer got three weeks, but it is immaterial.) A sentence like this, if given at the start and adhered to, would have been just. But they had already spent half a year in gaol, and they spent three more months there before they were sent back among other British prisoners. They only got out when they did by giving their parole. They had to give it. Probably they would otherwise have died or gone mad. Later on they withdrew their parole, got the withdrawal officially receipted this time, and one, if not more, of them escaped again and got clean away. Two of them are now back in the Navy. The other died in Turkey when the end of the war was in sight.

While we were in the church, Kut fell. Some of us could hardly believe it at first, especially those who had belonged to the 6th Division. It seemed too bad to be true. After what we had heard from those few who had already made the march from Mesopotamia to railhead, it was plain that the march of thousands of exhausted men along those desert ways would be a very terrible tragedy. But how terrible it was going to be I don't think even the men who had made it quite realized. The story of that march from Kut is not for me to write. But the impression that the arrival of the survivors made upon us earlier prisoners will be told in its time.

It was a long while yet before they reached us.

To me personally there came a great piece of news while we were in the church, for a letter dated a couple of months back told me that I was the father of a daughter. The telegram dispatched upon the same day reached me just three weeks after the letter. At that time I was singular in having so close a relation as yet unknown, but before the end came, as new prisoners dropped in, there were quite a band of us gaolbird fathers.

Beside the flagged path there were two Armenian tombs of some pretension, built of marble and carved with the usual imaginary fauna of heaven, all heads and wings. Further East, by the way, these things are flora, and grow on trees. They were crude affairs, of no interest except to their owners, but there was a space between them, and that was of interest to me. For, when the iron door was first opened in the morning, I used to come out and hide myself there and write verses. This is so largely a personal record that I make no apology for the recurrent references to my own method of killing care. It meant very much to me, as each man's method did to himself. In this quiet nook, before the path was thronged, I wrote a long description in verse of a Russian concert held in the church and of the riotous feast that followed it. Far from the riot I wrote it. But in the church itself, in the very vortex of hellish sound, I wrote a long poem on the great forests of Northern Ceylon. Far from peace, I wrote of the most peaceful place I know. And this paradox holds good, held good with me at least, all through. For in the next winter, with my feet in the Arctic and my head in the Tropics, with a freezing hand I used to write of that sunny land near the Equator. I believe it kept me warm.

Those hours before the multitude awakened were great hours. Even the smelly courtyard was attractive then. For one could look up from it, right up into the air, and see the great cliff that towered above the church turn gold in the light of the early sun. And the cliff was a great place for birds. Rock pigeons nested there in thousands, and swallows, and scores of beautiful little kestrels; and swifts flew, screaming out over the roofs below. Vultures brought forth their young there, whose first steps were on five hundred feet of empty air.

There is a rock in Ceylon very like the Kara-Hissar, a huge upstanding stump of granite called Sigiriya, the lion rock, and I had spent many happy months there, years before, delving into ruins of fourteen centuries ago. But the Kara-Hissar was good to look upon, apart from the memories it awakened, though memories are intensified in prison. In ordinary life one lives chiefly for the present: but in prison one lives almost entirely on the past and for the future.

It was not long before the pear trees came into blossom, and the white acacia. The sentries had kept us rigorously to the flagged path at first, while they used the garden space beneath the pear trees to grow a narrow bed of potatoes. But, either the potatoes failed, or they tired of the effort, for long before the end of our time there we used to walk freely to the outer edge, from where we could look down upon the town below. The Squire had received a drawing-book and a box of paints, and he used to make pictures there.

While we were in the church, before the potatoes had been abandoned, there was quite an exciting episode connected with an attempt at escape. The hero was a cheery Irishman, whom I will call Bart, the owner of one of the dogs, a beautiful Persian greyhound that he had acquired in Angora. He made up a bundle of food-stuffs and concealed it behind one of the Armenian tombs, where it would be handy when he required it, and so that he could come out of the church empty-handed and unsuspicious in appearance. But one of the guards noticed it, and a special sentry was put on to keep it under observation. It was obviously impossible to start like this, and for the time, at any rate, the attempt had to be abandoned. But it still remained to recover the precious pack and its contents. A Turkish sentry pretending not to watch anything is the most transparent thing in the world. It was easy to see what he was at: he wanted to identify the owner so that he might be cast into a dungeon. But it was not so easy to see how he was to be got rid of while the bag was removed. Bart was prepared to remove it rapidly inside a folding deck-chair, but he wanted an opportunity to grab it unawares. The sacred potatoes gave the key to the solution. I fetched Gumush, the greyhound, on a lead, and the perverse creature ran all over the cherished potatoes. As all the guards were co-partners in the garden, they all rushed to prevent the trespass; and the deed was done. In a moment, in the twinkling of an eye, that pack was safe in the church and its contents distributed. The sentry recovered his head, gave one look at the tomb, and made tracks for the Commandant's office. But we heard of it no more. The trap had failed, and the bait was gone.

I have mentioned the noise in the church, and it is only fair to tell of the music, real soul-stirring music. It was not made by the English; with a few exceptions they were not a musical lot as far as performance went. But the Russian sailors had a choir, and they sang like angels. It must have made the angels painted on the ceiling envious to hear them.

Their music was of a kind quite distinct from Western European music. Very sad and melancholy as a rule, in a minor key. Generally about eight of them would sing together, taking parts, but sometimes they would all join in, as when they held a sort of funeral service the night after their friend had died of typhus. And very few indeed of them could not sing. It used to put our own caterwauling concerts to utter shame. Most of them were simple, rather rough men; and though we knew them all as Russians in those pre-revolution days, I believe they really belonged to half a dozen different tribes; Cossacks, Ukrainians, Georgians, and Poles. But they could all sing. They sang the thing they called the Pan-Slav hymn. It is the forbidden national anthem of Poland, proscribed, before the war, in Russia, Austria, and Germany; and with equal fervour they sang the grand national anthem of Russia. "God Save the King" they sang, too, and made it sound magnificent. But for the most part they sang folk-songs. The song we liked the best was a beautiful Cossack lullaby. A fellow-prisoner has kindly written it out for me, and it is printed at the end of this chapter. The words given are some I wrote for it while in the church.

The singing of the Russians was the best thing there was in that church.

There were several Indians in Afion at that time, survivors of the Bagdad consular guard; and while we were in the church the last, or one of the last, died. When war broke out there was a guard of two Indian officers and about four-and-thirty soldiers attached to the Consulate. They were interned by the Turks. When disarmed they had all their kit complete, and they were in perfect physical condition. They were not half-famished when captured, like the garrison of Kut. They were not taken near the fighting line, where feelings ran high, as the rest of us were; on the contrary, the fighting line was hundreds of miles from them. But before the war ended every single one of those men was dead. They died of cold, calculated ill-treatment, starvation, and over-marching.

As I tell this tale, as I thread this rosary of months and years, there runs throughout a strand of the blackest tragedy, and it will come out, do what I can.

I am trying to put in all the funny things that happened, too, for there are things too sad to be serious about. But the tragedy is there, and it must be seen.

Still, it is a bad note to end a chapter on. As a crowd we were not downhearted, so I will pass to the tale of the frightened sailor man.

There was a certain sailor man who had heard strange tales about the Turks on his journeys round the world. He had heard how they bastinado men for small faults, and he had probably seen it, too; for at the time of which I write he was a captive in Turkey. In course of time, it happened that this sailor man, who was not a highly-educated person, was smitten with disease, as people in Turkey very often are. And, being at that time in a city, he was sent to a hospital. Now he did not know that typhus rages in the hospitals of the Turks, nor is it probable that he knew that this disease is conveyed by the bite of lice. If he had known this he would perhaps have been even more frightened than he actually was, and with far better cause.

One thing is quite certain, and that is that he did not know that all persons admitted to Turkish hospitals are clean-shaved all over. But he bore in mind many horrible stories, most of which were true, and, when a hospital orderly approached him with a razor in his hand, the sailor man's mind was invaded by the most terrible fear, for he had heard dreadful tales of the mutilations that Turks were said to practise upon their enemies. So he cried aloud with a great voice that it should not be done. And as for the explanations of the man with the razor, he heeded them not at all, for he knew no Turkish. Sooner would he die all at once, he cried, than be done to death piecemeal. And his cry was heard, for he prepared to fight, and the man with the razor did not want to fight him, nor did the doctor, nor did the assistant doctor. So in the end they sent to us for his own officer, who soothed his troubled mind until he allowed himself to be shaved.

THE RUSSIAN LULLABY

Shadows come a' creeping; Little stars are peeping;
Church bells distantly sound. Lie still, my babe, in your
cot gently sleeping, Dreaming while the world spins
round. Dream of your mother, her watch gladly
keeping, Smiling while the world spins round.
Through the curtains gleaming, Moonlight comes a'
beaming; Hush! My Baby, we're found. Deep in the
night the old moon sees you dreaming, Sleeping while
the world spins round. Bright kind old face, like a
sentinel seeming, Smiling while the world spins round.

Russian Lullaby

CHAPTER IX

THE LOWER CAMP

TOWARDS the latter end of May the great "strafe" ended. The Turks informed us that our punishment was fulfilled, and that we were to return to normal times again. For several days the senior officers of the different nationalities were very busy examining our new quarters and arranging matters generally, and then we began to move by masses out of the church. The French went first, to an Armenian house in the town. Soon afterwards the Russians followed to other houses in the same part of the Armenian quarter. And then the British officers, of whom there were now about forty, moved into a completely new block of jerry-built houses down by the station road. So new were the houses that the one I was in had no doors or windows when we went into it, and was not really completed the whole time we were there.

This block of four houses was known as the Lower Camp, for the Armenian quarter, or Upper Camp, was on higher ground and about a mile distant from it.

The Lower Camp consisted of a row of four houses under one continuous roof. Each house contained a kitchen and two rooms on the ground floor, as well as an open space in the centre, and three bedrooms upstairs, grouped round a central landing which served as a mess-room. The orderlies lived downstairs, and the officers upstairs, two in one small room at the back, and four in each of the two larger rooms in front.

Behind the houses was an open space, of rather over a quarter of an acre in extent, bounded by the backs of the houses on one side and by walls on the other three. This was known as the garden; for, when first we got there, it contained a couple of dozen cherry-trees about as big as walking-sticks. But these did not long survive, for a quarter of an acre is not a large playground for forty active officers and a dozen equally active orderlies, to say nothing of dogs and Turkish guards.

From the upper rooms we had wide views in both directions, out across the plain and far away into the distant hills. The front faced approximately south-east, and thirty miles away we could see the fine range of mountains known as the Sultan Dagh, capped with snow until far on into the summer. From the back windows we could see the Kara-Hissar, and a number of other rocky hills, like islands in the plain; and, in the distance, rolling hills and mountains one behind another. A good deal of the plain visible between the rocks was saline, and in early summer was blue with masses of a wild flower we knew as sea lavender.

It was really a beautiful view, especially in the spring, when the land was not so colourless as at other times. The soil of the plain was very soft and friable, and much dust used to hang in suspension, giving very vivid colours to the sunsets; sunsets of golden pheasants and peacocks' tails, and sunsets of red-hot copper. I have seen every shadow on the wall in the evening as blue as the bluest sea.

In the late summer great dust-storms used to roll up across the plain. We could see them gather on the distant hills, and come speeding towards us like banks of fog. And, as we hurriedly closed all the windows and fixed them tight, the storms would break upon the rocks, towering up high into the air in waves of brown, while the main body drove furiously towards us and lashed at the windows. A high wind would blow furiously for a few minutes, and then the storm would pass on across the plain, and rain would sprinkle the dust.

Some day that plain will be a great natural aerodrome, where people will halt on their way from Europe to the Far East.

The inhabitants of the house I was in, No. 3, were practically the same as in the house by the city wall in Angora. No. 1 was principally Mesopotamian, No. 2 chiefly the old Afion crowd, and No. 4 largely composed of the second Angora house. During the next two and a-half years many new prisoners came, and the old inhabitants had periodical times of restlessness when they shifted round, but the nuclei of the houses remained more or less constant, and the characteristic tone of each house remained practically unalterable. It is a very curious thing this tone or soul of each small subdivision of a community. I suppose every home in England has its own personal tone. Certainly each house in a public school has. Each ship has, and each regiment; and, in a larger way, each nation has, and will retain it despite Bolshevism.

We had not long been in the Lower Camp when new prisoners began to arrive. I cannot pretend to remember the order of their coming, for I kept no diary and have not a single note to help me; it does not, in any case, matter.

The yeomanry taken at Katia in the Sinai peninsula passed through on their way to a town in the north of Anatolia. We only had a glimpse of them as they passed; but we were able to supply them with a few books.

Other prisoners came in who stayed with us. The earliest to arrive were a very few who had been taken, one or two at a time, in the attempt to relieve Kut. One of these had been kept for several days in a small tent with a number of Arabs condemned to death. The Arabs were not allowed out of the tent for any purpose whatever.

Another had been chained to an Indian, and had dysentery while so chained. He and the Indian both got typhus, and the Indian died. After weeks in hospital the Britisher pulled through typhus, malignant malaria, and chronic rheumatism. He is now pulling through phthisis. Before that he had had sunstroke, and he was shot through the chest; not a bad record for a constitution to have pulled through.

Another British officer had been housed in the public gaol at Mosul, among the Turkish criminals, whose habits were so filthy that he asked to be allowed a privy to himself. His request was met by an order calculated to humiliate a clean Englishman in the eyes of the people of Mosul; for, after that, he was taken out each day by an armed guard and graciously permitted to make use of the street in the open bazaar. As I said before, Turks are a disgusting people.

Gradually, as more prisoners arrived, we overflowed into the Upper Camp. The Russians were sent away to another part of Anatolia, and their houses given over to British.

One other visit we had, from a German Staff-Colonel and several subordinates. "When will the war end?" we asked the great man.

"When we have taken Verdun," was his reply.

We had not much liberty at this time. A certain number of officers were allowed to go shopping on several days in the week. A piece of rocky ground was assigned to us to play cricket on. Each officer was allowed to go to the Turkish bath once a week. And once a week the camps visited each other.

For the rest, we had the garden, and the Upper Camp had a part of the street between their houses.

The chief game in the garden was a sort of badminton, played over a net with tennis rackets and balls made of stitched-up lumps of old sock. It went by the name of Bufru, coined by a cunning forger of Turkish.

But indoors there were many activities, both mental and physical. I should be afraid to say how many people wrote books. But the number of those who wrote plays must have been even greater. Some of them were very well produced. Several officers, notably one of the Australians, showed themselves to be quite expert designers of costumes, and most efficient needlemen. And some of the youngsters made very pretty women. The art of the female sex, in dressing as they do, was borne in upon me when I saw how quite plain young men could be made to look most attractive girls. **A** for a day, **B** for a week, and **C** for a life partnership, as someone wickedly compared the attractions of the three leading ladies. Some of the plays were very funny indeed, but the wit was not of that order which makes you pride yourself that you can see it. As a rule, it flew up and struck you all of a heap.

Another trial of the times was the debating society, in which all things on earth were discussed in due form, with a chairman, a proposer and seconder, an opposer and his second, a butter-in, and a ribald gallery. For days afterwards I used to hear the points argued and re-debated by the orderlies in the kitchen beneath my room. And two of the officers took themselves as future Public Men so seriously that they used to practise elocution on each other, each in turn suffering himself to be addressed by the other as "Gentlemen."

There were lectures, too, some of them very good ones. The subjects dealt with were catholic and included cocoanut-planting, Mendelism, flying, submarines, Singhalese history, Greek coins, Egyptian irrigation, and a host of other matters.

Besides these public efforts, there were men studying all manner of things in little cliques, or by themselves. One officer who knew no Arabic tapped Zaki to such good purpose that he (not Zaki) wrote an Arabic grammar. One old Australian of fifty, who had always lived, and would continue to live, in the back of beyond, studied simultaneously French, Norwegian, and Esperanto. There were teachers of mathematics, teachers of German, Tamil, Italian, Turkish and Russian. There were people teaching themselves to draw, or to play musical instruments. There were people studying law and medicine. I am sure that, at that time, we were the greatest centre of intellectual endeavour in the whole of the Turkish Empire.

In addition to the more purely intellectual occupations there were a number of really skilled carpenters, an officer who made himself an excellent little forge, where he turned out some very clever work, after having first manufactured the needful tools out of scrap steel; among them I remember a pocket-knife with various implements in it, and a stethoscope. The latter was for Bill.

Then there were cunning adorners of rooms, and still more cunning mixers of cocktails, in which a number of nauseous ingredients was made to taste good, as two negatives make an affirmative.

There were also breeders of dogs. Quite a rage there was for keeping dogs, on a quarter of an acre of land. Hilda and Gumush, the two original hounds of the Church days, presented their owners respectively with twelve and eleven puppies all in one week. At first it was very pretty to watch Bart training the young greyhounds, and teaching them to jump; he was a notable trainer of dogs. But when they all grew up, the overcrowding became intolerable. Public opinion revolted. Feelings were very deeply stirred, and people voted anti-dog or pro-dog, or pro-two-dogs, or pro or anti every possible combination and permutation of dogs. In the end the dogs were treated much as the Armenians. Some were slain, more were deported, and only three remained: Hilda, Gumush, and a funny little animal called Roger, who had a long body on the smallest legs, with the lowest gear, that I have ever seen.

In addition to dogs there were other pets: ducks, pigeons, chickens, enormous eagle-owls, a vulture, magpies, and finally a wolf. Cats were tried, but were somehow not a success.

There was also the native fauna. In my room I caught mice, voles, and shrews. Also smaller and more unpleasant creatures. Quite a feature of the spring awakening was the almost universal "bug-strafing" of beds. Our beds were all home made: a frame of pinewood, strung with thin rope, and carried on four legs. The joints and the holes where the rope passed through were the chief haunts of the foe. After breakfast, on a warm morning, officers in shirt sleeves, with kettles of boiling water and pots of Stockholm tar, might be seen carrying out that bold military measure known as a bug-strafe.

In summer I slung my bed by four ropes from the ceiling, and was fairly immune. They did not climb down the ropes, and they could not reach up from the floor, even standing on tip-toe. It was not only secure, but uncommonly comfortable.

Occasionally the Turks searched through our belongings to see if we had disguises, or diaries, or food stored for escape.

The first time they did it they caught us properly; but made an awful muddle of their triumph.

We were all ordered out into the garden, for what purpose we did not know; and, once out, sentries were placed at all the doors, and we were not allowed back again. But we asked as a favour that one cook in each house might be permitted to return, as otherwise our dinners would be spoiled. This was allowed. They began by searching No. 1 house, and as they were doing so our noble cook hid everything of any importance that he could lay hands on. Some under the charcoal, and some under the straw in Roger's kennel. Roger was very snappy with Turks, like all good dogs he detested them; and he sat tight on all my MSS. among other things. Everything in writing that a Turk cannot understand is to him abominable. What he can understand is rare above rubies.

Despite the efforts of the cooks, they did find a great deal of written matter, some of which it had been very unwise to keep: such things as diaries with descriptions of acts of atrocity in them, and plans for escape. There was nothing, so far as I ever heard, of the slightest military value. But there was a great deal that might have done us much harm. Perhaps the church over again. Fortunately the whole mass of literature was so enormous that it could not possibly be dealt with on the spot, so everything, plays, books, mess accounts, and the notes of study, as well as the more dangerous things, was stuffed into two or three sacks, and put in a small house in the garden. In addition to the sentry permanently in the garden, another, with a loaded rifle, was placed to guard the small house. This consisted of one room, with a barred window at one end, and a barred window and a locked door at the side. The side opposite to the door was blank, and was part of the garden wall. But the end facing No. 4 house had a tiny window in it which had no bars. There were no blinds to any of the windows, and the sentry had only to look in to see that the sacks were still there.

The matter was very serious indeed. There was some very incriminating stuff there, and we did not at all desire another two months of the church. All sorts of measures were proposed and rejected. Burning the whole place down was mooted, but decided to be impossible, for paper burns so slowly that the sacks would certainly be saved. Then Bart did a very daring thing. He had slim shoulders, but a great heart, and he thought his narrow body might squeeze through the unbarred window. He waited an opportunity and dived through. Once in, squatted on the floor, the sentry would have to come right up to the window in order to see him. But the sentry only watched the door. And while he watched, Bart went through the lot as swiftly as a post office sorter, and removed more than half of the most dangerous items. He got safely out again, while the sentry still watched the door.

In No. 3 house, an officer named Budd was less fortunate. Trying to explain that he wanted to keep the mess accounts, he lost his temper and damned the interpreter. He was at once searched personally, and sent away into the town, where he was confined in a cellar. When he asked for bread, the gaoler said, "Para yok, ekmek yok," which means, "No money, no bread." Fortunately, Budd had money; but he had a very unpleasant five or six days before he was released. In the cell next to his he heard a poor, miserable little Chaldean priest, who had bravely but unwisely kept some record of the Armenian girls enslaved in various Turkish families, being mercilessly flogged, and screaming in his agony.

Bart had collected some of the diaries, but there were still others, and at least one plan of escape most unwisely committed to writing. A community would be incomplete without its salt of folly.

A few days later the remaining documents returned to us too. The Turks had bungled over the cooks, bungled over guarding their spoil, and now they bungled again worse than ever. They had a positive genius for incompetency: a masterly faculty for determining the wrong way to do a thing, and for doing it. After a few days, a sack of papers and note-books was returned to the camp. To our surprise, it was found to contain all those documents which we had feared the Turks might discover and keep.

But the puzzle was elucidated by a letter which followed, a rather abject letter from the interpreter, stating that he had returned the wrong sack by mistake, and, if we would not tell the Commandant of his error, would now send us the right one! So we recovered everything.

In the Upper Camp they were not so lucky. There, the Turks adopted the simple method of destroying all written matter. It was things like that which made it so difficult for officers to keep any account of the treatment of their men.

The only person, besides Budd, who suffered actual penalty from this raid, so far as I remember, was the celebrated French cook, late of the Jockey Club. He had kept a diary, and in it had stupidly written the use to which he thought the Turkish flag should be put by a French sailor. It might be thought, after some of our treatment, that this was merely tit-for-tat, six of one and half a dozen of the other. As a fact, it was twelve dozen of one and very gross of the other. So the French cook went to gaol, and we saw him in Afion no more.

In this gallery of portraits I think Porter is more than worthy of mention. He was an orderly in No. 4 house, a slight, fair-haired young fellow from the Isle of Wight. Before the war he had been a barber, and he used to cut our hair and trim our beards: for many of us grew beards. But his claim to fame was that he was the most wounded man in Afion. In an attack on Gallipoli he had been shot through the body, and while lying on the ground had been terribly wounded again by shrapnel. To finish him off the Turks had cut his head open with a shovel, and bayoneted him many times. He had in all twenty-one wounds. But he resolutely refused to die, and when last I saw him was as merry as a cricket, and able to play quite a good game of football. I sometimes wonder how many wound-stripes he is entitled to, and whether he is trying to grow fat enough to wear them all. He told me once that what he disliked most was being stabbed in the stomach; and he certainly is an authority to be respected.

Having no diary, I shall certainly not tempt critics by trying to fix a date for the total eclipse of the moon. But one occurred while I was in the lower camp, some time between June of 1916 and November of 1917. It was either just before or just after the entry of Greece into the war. Elston and I, who occupied a small room at the back of the house, had gone to bed early and were nearly asleep when we were roused by repeated firing away in the town. We sat at the window and watched flash after flash; some in the streets, some on the hill-side, and some apparently from the windows. There were the shots of modern rifles, of revolvers, and the duller boom of old-fashioned muzzle-loading guns. We thought at first it was brigands attacking the town. Then we remembered the Greeks, and we feared that a great massacre had begun, for there were many Greeks in Afion. They must be putting up a good fight, we thought, as we listened to the continuous crackling, and watched the flashes. So we went across the mess-room to see if the others in the front rooms, had heard it, too. We found them all gathered at the windows, watching the eclipse of the moon. The whole town was blazing away at the dragon who was swallowing the moon. In the road before the house our sentries stood anxiously, all blazing away Government ammunition in the good cause; ammunition that was meant for us. They just flung their rifles to their shoulders and opened rapid fire, loaded up, and did it again.

In No. 2 house there was an officer who had lived for years in Turkey and knew the language well; so, when the N.C.O. in charge of the guard addressed his troops, we had a ready interpreter. "We are all ignorant men," said the chaous. "I am ignorant myself. But I know that the moon has not gone for ever. It will return. Still, I don't like that blood-red colour, so fire away." And they did.

CHAPTER X

THE SECOND YEAR

TO a large extent, the events chronicled in the last chapter overlap into the second year. Some have been recorded as the natural sequels to others, and some generalisations cover the whole of captivity. But, broadly speaking, I am trying to make the record as continuous as possible, and to preserve chronological order.

We had been in Turkey for less than a year when we first established code correspondence with England. All our letters were censored in Vienna as well as in Constantinople, and perhaps locally; but, so far as we know, our code was never discovered. It was suspected, at least, some means of communication was suspected, because the Turkish Government was requested, through the Dutch Embassy, to set right certain urgent wrongs, and they knew that some one of us must have reported those wrongs. Letters frequently used to arrive with the marks of a hot iron on them, showing that they had been tested for at least one form of invisible writing. There are many forms of invisible writing, but we did not use them. We used a plain, straightforward code, and our letters might have been read by anyone on earth. It was curious that none of us should have arranged a code before leaving home, but no one had, and I never yet met a prisoner who had even contemplated the idea of being captured.

Since our correspondence, after passing through several hands and various different addresses in England, eventually reached the War Office, it is obviously impossible for me to describe it. But I should like, however anonymously, to pay a tribute to the clever person who received the first code letter, realized that it was code, discovered the key to it, knew what to do with it, and acted as our central post office for the two and a-half years. He (she) had no idea that a code message was coming, and had no clue beyond what his (her) brain afforded.

It is a pleasure, too, to be able to claim that, though immobilized, we were not altogether useless.

What exactly they would have done with us if they had brought home to us a charge of conveying information of military value, I do not know. The most probable fate would have been a dungeon until the end of the war, or for as long as one could stand it. But, though I am unable to make further reference to the system we actually used, it may not be completely without interest to give an example of what can be done in the simplest possible way. For instance, a prisoner writes the following letter:—

DEAR ELIJAH

It is four months now since you wrote to me about the proposed division of Dad's property, and I have not had a single line since. If I am passed over because I am away it will be very hard, through no fault of my own. I don't think that Gwendoline will be greedy enough to treat me as you say. And anyhow I rely upon you to do your best to bag the old hall clock for me. Dear old Dad always meant it for me, and it seems only yesterday that he promised me it, &c. &c.

That is simple enough. It would pass any censor. But it contains military information. It is not the code we used, but it was, as a matter of fact, one which was held in reserve as a possibly useful one. It was never communicated home.

Read it again in the light of the key, which is the Greek letter π. Every schoolboy knows π. It is something or other to do with the relation of a circle's circumference to its diameter. I am no mathematician, but I know that π means 3·14159. Take the third word of the first line, the first of the second line, the fourth of the third line, and so on right through the letter following π. It will then read: "Four division passed through to Bag Dad yesterday."

In addition to writing codes, I took to studying cypher, and of all the nine or ten varieties of cypher given me by various prisoners never found one for which a method of solution could not be worked out. An average piece of Playfair took me about three and a-half hours: probably an expert would do it in half that time. This is not written as an advertisement for the study of cypher, but to show the straits to which a prisoner may be driven for want of occupation. Few occupations are more detestable than poring over cypher, but total inaction is worse. It is an occupation for a slave, and now I am no longer a slave I hope never to do it again.

Enough has been said of prisoners' occupations now for the rest to be left to imagination. Here endeth the Arts and Crafts section.

Towards the end of the summer of 1916 some of the generals taken in Kut passed through Afion. None of them made more than one night's stop there. But after them there came some officers who did stop; and from them we heard how the men had suffered on their deadly trek over the desert. The road from Bagdad to Aleppo is strewn with the bones of the British and Indian soldiers of Kut. We used to see gangs of men arrive and walk up from the station to the town, almost too weak to look up at our windows as they passed. And hundreds, thousands, have died or been killed on the way, long before they reached Afion. At Afion itself they were not badly treated then, but they reached that comparative refuge so weak and worn out that very many of them died there. We used to see their bodies by twos and threes and half-dozens being carried to the Armenian cemetery where they were buried. We were not allowed to go to their funerals, but later, when we had a padre, he was allowed to read the burial service over the Christians.

The senior British officer was allowed a little, a very little, communication with the men. The other officers were allowed none at all. But through our shopping orderlies we kept in touch with them. Those shopping orderlies became masters of intrigue. I am sure that each successive senior officer did every single thing that he could for the men. It was uphill work the whole way through. The unfortunate officer who had to deal direct with the Turkish officials found himself baffled at every point by lies, and lies, and lies; by cheating and by bare-faced robbery. Whatever he could do he did do, but it was absolutely heart-breaking. Thank goodness, I was a very junior officer, and one who trembled in the presence of more than three stars.

I have been to that cemetery, not so very bad a place as cemeteries go. There is a stone wall round it, and in it are a number of Armenian tombstones of white marble. Many of them have carved upon them little pictures of the implements proper to the deceased's trade: scissors for a tailor, a hammer and a chisel for a stonemason, and so forth. A very large number bear the image of a small basin with a very fat caterpillar in it. I thought it was the worm which dieth not, but others have held it to be a chalice containing the spirit of the departed rising in vapour.

It was a sad place, and many good fellows lie there, both officers and men, who need not have died.

Afion was looked upon by the Turks as a rest camp. The church and the Medrisseh were used as barracks for the sick and for worn-out prisoners. But when the men gained strength again they were sent out in working parties: some to cut timber in the forests near the Black Sea, some to work on the railway then being built through the Taurus mountains, and some even beyond the Taurus. There were good places and there were bad; and in the worst of them life was Hell, and death came swiftly.

The only prisoner we ever had who had been a prisoner in Germany too during this war—he had escaped from there and been recaptured—said that the difference in treatment between the worst places in Germany and Turkey was this: in Germany the men were ill-treated until they became ill, and were then put into hospital; in Turkey they were ill-treated until they became ill, and were then ill-treated more until they died. Before the end we used to reckon, so far as we could get smuggled figures, that seventy-five per cent. of all men who had been taken prisoners two years or more earlier were dead. Three out of every four. It was not only the Kut prisoners who had gone on short rations before they were captured. It was all the prisoners, all those who were not officers. For the Turks thought that if they sent back to England most of the officers, no inquiry would be made about the men by the British nation, any more than, in the opposite case, the Sublime Porte would have seriously objected. I have met people who thought it was only the Kut prisoners who were ill-treated, but, once that tragic march across the desert was over, the prisoners from Kut, officers and men alike, mixed with the other prisoners from all the other fronts and were in no way distinguished from them, either by the Turks or by themselves.

There were places where working parties were treated well. We heard the most extraordinary tales of places where British N.C.O.'s were running the whole show themselves, running the prisoners and running the Turks too: men who had come to the top by sheer force of character. It is very greatly to be hoped that some account of this will see daylight. I wish the details were in my hands. But these places were rare. There were other hells upon earth where the men were beaten and starved, robbed of the money sent them from home, robbed of their parcels, frozen in the winter and overdriven in the summer until they died, either from sheer collapse or from one of the many diseases that a dirty country breeds.

People who have no special knowledge of Turkey-in-Asia hardly realize what the winter is like there. The last winter we were in Afion snow fell at the end of November and did not melt until the middle of March. The temperature ranged round about zero for a good many weeks. What this meant to the men in some of the bad places can easily be imagined. Clothes were provided for them by our Government, acting through the Protecting Embassy; but, except where British officers were stationed and were permitted to issue them, these clothes were nearly always stolen. So were their boots. One of the orderlies in the house I was in latterly had twice been to hospital—before he became an orderly—and each time he had been looted of every stitch he possessed and of his boots. Both times he had to start again in Turkish rags.

It is not my aim to complain about the lot of the officers. We were lucky to be alive, and we did not really have a very bad time. But most of the men were so unlucky that they are now dead, and while they lived they suffered all manner of ill.

This book would indeed be incomplete were I to fail to tell of the plight of the men.

I expect they are forgetting it. People do forget things.

But I must go back to our own history, the history of the Lower Camp in 1916-17.

That winter was a mild one. We played football about two or three times a week on a small ground about half a mile from the camp. Association was the rule that year, but the following winter we played Rugby. The football ground was a long, rather narrow strip between two ploughed fields, and the reasons it was not ploughed up were two. It sloped toward the road, and all the lower portion was used as a threshing floor at harvest time. The Turkish method of threshing is a very remarkable one, very early, I imagine. When the straw stacks have ripened sufficiently they are broken up, and large circular mats of straw with the grain in it are arranged upon the ground. On these mats sleds made of three planks, and, drawn by horses, are driven round and round, as though in a circus. Under the sleds are grooves containing rows of sharp flints which cut all the straw up into chaff and separate the grain from the husk. Then the whole mass is winnowed in the wind, and divided into two heaps, one of food for man and the other of food for beasts. Which of the two our bread was made of I forget.

This threshing naturally requires a good deal of space, and it protected the lower part of our football field. The upper half was conserved in quite a different way, for it was a Hebrew cemetery.

There was a large slab or soft rock in it, roughly squared and conveniently situated for those who wished to watch the game.

Three of us were sitting on this one day when a Turk, driving a cart along the road, turned his horse and drove up to this stone. He asked us to move to one side, and then gravely led the horse three times round the stone, after which he dug out a piece of earth from under the stone and gave it to the horse to eat. The only thing we could get out of him was that the horse was ill and that it would now get well. To prove his point he beat it all the way back to the road and made it canter. There was only one thing remarkable about the stone, and that was that it was pierced all over by nails hammered in, nails of all shapes and sizes, and some of them entirely rusted away, leaving only a stained hole. But just think of the plight of that poor horse! Officially speaking, it was now well, registered as A1. Any further weariness would be put down to malingering, and treated accordingly.

In the spring of 1917 we began to get a little more liberty. For some time the Commandant answered all applications to be allowed to go out for walks by saying that the weather was not yet fine enough, a subterfuge so transparent that I suspect he was laughing at us. His sense of humour was a very grim one. He appeared one morning and told the senior officer that three British soldiers were to be hanged that day. Of course there was a vigorous protest made; but, after a while, the Commandant smiled and went away. He then visited the senior French officer and told him that three Frenchmen were to be hanged. After he had enjoyed his joke sufficiently, it came out that three Turks actually were hanged on that day. There was nobody to protest for them, poor devils! The Turkish method of hanging is to erect a tripod, rather like a strong, high camera-stand. The victim stands below the centre of this, a noose is passed round his neck, and the legs of the tripod are pushed closer and closer in until the man is lifted from the ground and strangled. The men at the Medrisseh often saw public execution take place, I believe.

But when spring grew fine enough we actually did go for several long walks, and saw the little yellow crocuses thrusting their heads up on the hill-sides. It was good to see flowers grow again. The wild flowers were wonderful round Afion. But that spring we saw little of them. The policy was changed again, and instead of being allowed out for walks in the country, we were allotted a little corner of one of the hills overlooking the town. Here we used to march, twice a week, and sit for an hour or two on the grass. It was steep and rocky, and there was nothing else to be done there. People used to take books out there, or pencils and paper and try to draw the one view. Then we would walk back to tea, through the slums of Afion, down narrow roads, past huts and graveyards, past kitchen middens where dead cats' and horses' skulls lay, and where children played: sturdy, grimy little urchins who used to abuse us, and make their favourite cutthroat sign, drawing their baby hands across their necks.

I forget when the policy was changed again. It was always being changed. Capricious and wavering as thistledown. But in the summer we had quite a lot of liberty. We used to gather huge armfuls of purple larkspur, pink orchis, and yellow dog-roses. It was a good time for most of us, but early in the summer five officers were suddenly taken from their friends and shut up in a separate house in the Armenian quarter. They were allowed a short time twice daily for exercise in about 50 yards of the street, but for the rest were no better off than if they were in gaol. They were not released until about Christmas time. All this was because the Commandant suspected them of planning to escape.

The Upper Camp grew a great deal larger that year. All the Russians came back again, and with them a great many more Russian officers who had been interned at Sivas for several years previously. From Yozgat, too, a large number of British officers came, among whom were two of the three who had escaped in March, 1916. From being a camp of one British house and one French, the Upper Camp now spread the whole length of one street, and into two neighbouring by-streets. The whole community of prisoners in that camp lived in Armenian houses.

My personal opinion is that the camps as a whole lost interest a great deal after this. They certainly became more respectable, but the character of the place altered. It improved on the whole, but it was duller. In the old days we had at least this in common, that we were all different; we had all come into Turkey in different ways and at different times. Now that queer distinction disappeared, for most of the new-comers were from Kut, the senior officers in nearly all of the houses were from Kut, and Kut rather dominated the conversation. We old-timers were a little sick of Kut. They were mostly old regular soldiers, and senior to the rest of us. Let me hasten to say that I have never met a nicer lot of men. That was part of the difficulty. They were nicer than we were. But they had all led the same sort of lives before the war, and during the war. They had all fought in the same battles, and been in the same siege. They had all the same adventure to tell. I have great friends among them, and I hope they will smile if ever they read this. But the old-timers will smile, too, and recognize the truth that is in me.

One result of this influx was that we all became very unsettled. The fact was that we had stagnated too long, and were growing very queer. We were used to new prisoners dropping in one or two at a time, and trying to teach us how to be prisoners. We knew how to be prisoners; we had learned it in a bitter school; so we smiled at these new babes in the wood, let them kick against the pricks a little, and took them to our bosoms. They made no difference. But you can't take old regular lieutenant-colonels to your bosom, you have to wait until they take you to theirs. They do in time, at least these did. But they unsettled the whole place, and it was probably very good for us.

The result was a break up of many happy homes, a great deal of arrangement and rearrangement of houses, and when we settled down again it was like a new Parliament with a different cleavage of parties, and a strange Government.

At the end of all this I found myself in the Upper Camp, in a house of twelve almost equally divided between Kut and non-Kut. It was a very happy house. I don't think anyone in it really hated any of the others; and, in prison, that means that you like each other very much, and will always be glad to meet each other again for the rest of your lives.

It was a very respectable house. Much too respectable to be popular. Indeed it was a byword for respectability, until Good Friday, 1918; but that is anticipating.

We thought, a lot of us, that the war was going to end that year, so who can say that we were downhearted?

CHAPTER XI.

THE LAST YEAR IN AFION

AN accurate description of all our ups and downs, of liberty enlarged and liberty snatched away again, and of all the fluctuating fortunes of the camp would be as dull as our lives were, and as little likely to be voluntarily undergone as was our captivity. That gem of time cannot be polished in all its facets, lest the observer should be dazzled. All that will be attempted here is some account of the main events. Another man, looking at that time from a different angle, might write a book that would hardly parallel this upon a single point, and yet be as true a picture.

We were all growing very weary indeed of being prisoners. Prices had continued their inexorable rise, and frequent mass meetings were held to discuss ways and means, for of course there were poor among us who could not afford to get money sent from home, and the pace of the convoy had to be that of the slowest ship. The only alternative would have been to break up into houses where men lived by bread alone, and houses where plutocrats resided who were able to import money at the disastrous rates obtainable. For it cost a very large sum to import money. A cheque on an English bank for £20 would produce a draft of £Tq.26. This would be paid in paper, and to find its true value must be divided by six; so by spending £20 a prisoner could obtain the value of £4 6s. 8d.[2]

Of course we did import money, whatever it cost, even the poorest of us practically had to, unless he would freeze in the winter. The actual necessaries of life, food, fuel, and clothes of sorts, were always obtainable in Turkey; at a price. The country was so completely unorganized, and the railway so congested that food-stuffs might be plentiful in one district and almost unobtainable in another not far away. But where the food was grown it was always obtainable, and fortunately for us, Afion was in an agricultural district.

The winter of 1917-18 was a very severe one. Late in November the street that was our only playground and space for exercise was filled with snow. It ran east and west, overhung by a steep hill on the south, and deprived of sun by the opposite row of houses. No sunlight at all reached that street for quite three months, and during the whole of that time it was paved with snow that had been trodden hard.

There were refugees in the town that winter, people of strange appearance to us who were used to the Turks. They were said to be Kurds mostly, but there were certainly several tribes represented. For some reason or other they had been evacuated from some part of the Turkish Empire further east, and dumped down at Afion. Their clothes were those of a warm climate, and many of the little children had but one thin garment apiece. Nominally, I expect, they were supposed to be fed by their predatory Government: actually they were on or over the verge of starvation. We used to see them from our windows, and on our comparatively rare passages through the town.

There is no sanitation in a Turkish town. All refuse is cast upon middens, which in the course of ages become great mounds. Houses do not last long in Turkey; they are but flimsily built and fires are very frequent. They decay or are destroyed by fire, and they are rebuilt upon these middens. I picked up a Roman coin once where a midden had been disturbed, for they are very old.

And one of the uses of these middens is to provide food for the utterly poor. These poor refugees used to haunt those hideous piles of decaying matter and pick food from them. Dogs and donkeys, children and buffalo calves, old women and cats, used to scramble and scrape for the last pieces.

We had a Rugby football that winter, and in a field by the river, another of the wide threshing floors, we began to play when the snow melted. There were some very good players, and we had one new prisoner who held, and I believe still holds, the 'Varsity record for both the 100 yards and the quarter-mile. There were several matches, and one very great triumph, when The Dardanelles played The World and beat it. There were so few to pick from that I played for the Dardanelles. Until that winter, the last game I had played was in Ceylon in 1902; and I went to bed for three days after the match. But we, the old-timers, beat the World and rejoiced exceedingly.

One other thing that happened that winter must be told, though it is painful to write it. There was a Russian named Constantine B., who had become estranged from the other Russians for a fault of his own. He was afterwards forgiven, and taken back, so it would not become me to say anything about it. For the time, however, he lived separately in a small house with a Russian anarchist and a Russo-Armenian thief, and the three of them were outlaws. Also they hated each other, and used to quarrel. One of their quarrels became acute enough to attract the attention of the Turkish Commandant, the infamous Maslûm Bey, who visited their house to make inquiries, and there lost his temper and struck Constantine B. Constantine was not really a bad fellow. He had done one bad thing, but he was out of place in that house. He was a man of about thirty, tall, well built, with very fair hair. A brave man, and quick-tempered. He put up his arm to protect himself, and he was lost. The Commandant accused him of trying to reach for his, the Turk's, sword, and had him arrested.

Constantine B. was taken away from the officers' camp to the church where were some British soldiers; in the little courtyard where we used to box he was stripped and tied head downwards with his feet in the air. The Commandant stood by while Constantine was beaten upon the soles of the feet with raw hide whips until he fainted. An hour later he was beaten again until he lost consciousness once more. As they grew tired the Commandant called new hands to beat him; every Turk there had a turn at beating him. And, when he could feel no more, Maslûm Bey kicked and struck him all over, everywhere on his body, and spat upon him. Then he was taken into a dungeon and thrown upon a heap of quicklime where his face got burnt.

Maslûm's cup was not yet full. Constantine recovered in time, though he is lame. Maslûm went on to his worst offence. He had flogged our men and the Russians. He had imprisoned British officers in filthy holes, for little or no cause. He had lied, and swindled, and stolen, and grown rich. He now proceeded to overstep even the line which a Turkish officer draws. All through the writing of this book there has loomed ahead of me the grave difficulty of dealing with Maslûm Bey's greatest offence. It ought to be recorded, but I loathe doing it. Let those who can read between the lines. Some of the British soldiers were very young, fair-haired Saxon boys from Wessex. They had seen a vast deal of cruelty, and they knew how easy it was for Maslûm Bey to flog them, even to kill them, or to send them to places where they would almost certainly die. Four of these became the victims of the abominable wickedness of Maslûm. Under the shadow of a raw hide whip, in the hands of Turkish non-commissioned officers, they were his victims.

All these offences of Maslûm Bey, from the tragedy of Constantine downwards, were duly reported to England by code. The very names of the offences were squeezed into that code. I had the pleasure of sending the messages myself, and the framing of them. They got home safely, and our Government acted at once.

In the end we got rid of Maslûm Bey. He was court-martialled by a commission of utterly corrupt Turkish officers. The British soldiers bravely told their stories. I say bravely, for their lives hung by a hair. A British officer who knew Turkish equally bravely conducted the prosecution for our side; and his life hung by a hair too. But we got rid of Maslûm Bey. He was given five and a-half months' simple imprisonment. Not six months, for that would have involved loss of rank. His judges did not think he had deserved to lose rank.

That is why I watch the papers to see if Maslûm Bey has been hanged.

We used to stick up for ourselves in Turkey. At one time I knew how many commandants of prison camps were broken by the British in three and a-half years. But my memory is a prison-memory. It is like fishing in a well-stocked stream with a torn landing-net. When you have got a fish, there you see him plain enough; but more often you see but a gleam, and he is gone. The first Commandant of Afion was broken for swindling; the second broke himself by letting prisoners escape; the third was Maslûm Bey; and the fourth was a gentleman. British prisoners broke one Commandant at Kastamouni, and I believe another at Broussa, Russians broke one at Kutahia. And down the line, in the Taurus or beyond it, where there were no British officers, I believe our men broke more than one.

After Maslûm had gone we were very well treated. I don't think that any prisoners could have expected to have a juster man to deal with than our new Commandant, Zeir Bey. Just think what an opportunity of regeneration Turkey lost in this war. Had the Ottoman Government selected men like Zeir Bey to command each camp, they would have made friends for themselves not only all over the British Empire, but in France and her colonies, in Russia, in Italy and in Rumania. Instead of which they have made bitter enemies.

Our Indians had the greatest contempt and hatred for the Turks, all but a few who were traitors. There were some, a few, real traitors among the Indians; but there were many more who are much more to be pitied than blamed for some of the things they did. Their position was an exceedingly difficult one. Very many of them died, thousands of them; but the Turks were always trying to seduce them from their allegiance. There was even a paper printed in Hindustani by the Germans and given free to the Indians. The Sultan sent for Indian Mohammedan officers and gave them swords. One sturdy Pathan, Kutab Gul, went to prison rather than accept a sword. For the most part the Indians were kept at different stations from the British, at Konia and other places where they could get no guidance from their British officers, where no one knew their tongue, and where they could get no news of the war except such as was faked, and the usual bazaar rumours. And this went on for years. As they would themselves admit, Indian officers are in some respects very child-like people. They believe a lot of what they hear. We had our own means of communication outside, and we knew how to read between the lines of German *communiqués*. Also we could read French, and in Turkey there are many papers printed in French for the polyglot peoples of the Eastern Mediterranean. But the Indians had none of these means. For instance, if we read "The enemy attacked near Braye and was heavily defeated. By their self-abnegation our brave umteenth regiment of Bavarians threw the enemy back with bloody losses," we knew what it meant. It was the obituary notice of the umteenth Bavarians, who had been wiped out. If the *communiqué* went on to say, "Our line, according to a pre-arranged plan, now stretches from X to Y," we knew just how far the Germans had retreated. If our maps did not show the places, someone among the officers, either British or French, generally knew them. But how were the Indians to know that? They learned Turkish and read the Turkish papers, but that was no good. The Turkish method of camouflaging news is not the same as the German. It is better. They just say nothing. They never admitted the fall of Bagdad. They just kept on saying nothing. So skilled were we in interpreting the German news that I really believe we knew just as much about the war as the average officer outside. Our naval officers reconstructed the Battle of Jutland, boomed as a great German victory, so accurately that the real account we got at last seemed stale news. We certainly knew more about the war than the Turkish officers did locally; and they used to come and look at our great war maps drawn out on a large scale by Capt. Sandes, R.E., from innumerable scraps and pieces out of newspapers.

Sandes did three things. He wrote a book upon the Mesopotamian campaign, now with a publisher. He made maps, and he was the bandmaster. Among the later prisoners there were a number of musicians, and at least one really ambitious composer who wrote many songs and an oratorio. There were three violins and a guitar in the orchestra, and there used to be excellent Sunday concerts in the Yozgat house at the top of the street, which was our Albert Hall. There were also several prisoners who sang really well. This last year saw a great renaissance in the theatrical world too. There was a revolt against the bondage of the old border-line jokes, and an attempt to substitute wit for wickedness. The men in the church used to get up plays, too. Maslûm Bey was a great patron of the theatre, and would save the best actors from being sent away on working parties. He used to bring parties of veiled Turkish women to watch their plays from the gallery. Behind the altar were dark passages on either side, built in the thickness of the wall, and well adapted for the wings of the stage. What he liked best were love scenes, and he used to send down messages in the middle of the acting commanding the performers to make love more briskly.

With the passing of Maslûm we came to the end of our worst troubles. The new Commandant was not so incurably Asiatic. He realized that prisoners, like other men, love life, and freedom, and the open sky. That summer we had a wide and high hill-side made free to us. We could spend the whole day there if we liked. The Lower Camp had an even better recreation ground in a rocky hill just beyond their houses. We were allowed out in smaller parties and for longer distances. Smaller parties was a very great gain, for to walk out in a "crocodile" is so unpleasant that it is almost better to stay indoors. We used to get a sentry, and go off into the hills with our lunch, and picnic all day. And as we could go in several directions there was not much crowding. There was fishing in the stream, and bathing in a big pool, and sketching along the valley above the pipe-line. It was by far the best time we ever had in Turkey, and all because England and her Allies were winning the war. For it certainly was that consideration which caused them to send us Zair Bey.

Among the prisoners there were some who said, "When we win the war the Turks will massacre us all." But those among us who knew the East said, "When we win the war the Turks will lick our boots and feed out of our hands." We were right. Had we *lost* the war it would have been quite another matter, and this history would never have been written.

It was different now from the old days when Toomy and I used to sit by a charcoal brazier and plan revenge. Our great scheme was to introduce rabbits into Anatolia: the country was suitable, and they were to overrun the whole land, worse than in Australia, and eat up all the young crops. We also thought of water hyacinth in the Tigris and Euphrates. But we were winning the war now, and these guerilla operations would not be necessary. But we never thought the end was as near as it proved.

CHAPTER XII

OUR ALLIES

WHILE in Turkey I only saw Italian prisoners once. They were locked into railway wagons, and when they tried to peer out through the barred windows a German N.C.O. brutally thrust at their faces with his stick. They were stated to have elected to come to Turkey rather than to remain in Austria, where food was short. They were on their way to work in a mine in the vilayet of Aidin.

At one time there were a good many Serbs in Afion, but we saw very little of them. Those I saw were apparently dying of starvation but they seemed to be cheerful folk.

There were nine French officers at Afion, and, except for one who spent a long time in a Constantinople hospital, they were with us the whole time. They and the English were on the best of terms throughout, and they were a very nice lot of fellows indeed. They were most studious people and only one of them wrote a book. One of them, however, read through Gibbon's "Decline and Fall" three times, besides devouring every other history he could obtain, and we had many books. We had a large library of general fiction, recruited from parcels, and we had a fairly large reference library of solid works, partly from parcels and partly from the Education Department at home. And, between them, the French must have read nearly all of those hundreds of books, ranging from "The Way of an Eagle" to Mahan's "Sea Power."

The French were extraordinarily generous, too, in giving up their time to teach their language to Englishmen. Very few, if any, of them had not several English pupils, and one ran a large class. With only one exception they could all speak English fluently long before most of us learned much French.

Our pronunciation was, of course, a mystery to them, nor was it to be wondered at. Their house was too large for them alone, and Britishers who wished to study French joined their mess. They had at one time Australians, a Canadian, a Lancashire man, and a Scot, and each of them spoke English in a different way. No wonder the French found it difficult.

For a whole year once the French were not allowed out farther than that strip of street, sunless and frozen in the winter, dusty in the summer, and crowded all the year round. The pretext was a reprisal for some imagined wrong done to Turkish prisoners in France. We suffered from a continual threat of reprisals like this. Six Englishmen were once imprisoned for months in a loathsome hole in Constantinople for some crime of our Government, probably invented, and one of the six died as a result. And there were other minor cases of the same kind. It is useless for a civilized people to swap reprisals with savages: the savages will win every time.

The French temperament was totally different from the English. They used to get extraordinarily elated at times, and at other times they became desperately depressed. We did both of these things too, but our pendulum was longer and did not swing so suddenly. In the great German offensive of the spring of 1918 we refused to be downhearted. "They will take Paris!" the French would cry. "Very likely," we would reply; "perhaps we are leading them on." There was unpleasantness over this kind of divergence, and they would say despairingly, "Oh! you bloody English! You do not understand." But no real quarrel ever resulted. The most frequent offender was an Irish major, who assiduously studied French. His joy was to lead his tutor to the verge of hysterics by calculated callousness regarding German victories. The poor tutor would scream at him, but they were really the best of friends. "Unless I rouse him," the major would say, "he won't speak fast enough to give me the practice in conversation that I require."

I shall never forget a scene in the church, where, by the way, the French beat us at all points in quiet endurance of a detestable experience. A certain French officer resented having his belongings searched, and certain articles of Turkish clothing "stolen" from him. In revenge he shaved off his moustache, fitted a large newspaper cocked hat upon his head, and strutted fiercely up and down the central aisle, looking the very personification of *revanche*. He was a tiny man, very clever, and a great mathematician. Why he did it the Lord alone knows, but he did; and he felt as one embarking upon a forlorn hope. There was not a smile in the affair—on his side—from beginning to end.

The French senior officer was a very fine man, one of the best-read and all-round best-informed men I have ever met, and he ran his rather difficult mixed French and British house tactfully and well.

Utterly different were the Russians. To begin with, a great many of them were not prisoners of war at all, but the officers and engineers of Black Sea trading vessels. These unfortunates had not been allowed to leave Constantinople when they wished to, about a week before war was declared, and they were older prisoners than any of us. "Comme vous êtes jeune!" said one to me when I told him I had just completed my third year. He had done nearly four. Then they belonged to many nationalities, some of them peoples one had hardly heard of before the war: Ukrainians, Lithuanians, Poles, Polish Jews, Cossacks, Georgians, Russian Armenians,

Russian Greeks, Russian Italians, Great Russians and Little Russians, and others I forget.

Their senior officer was a Commander in the Black Sea fleet, a very nice, quiet, friendly man of about fifty. He had lost every single thing in the world except the few articles of clothing remaining to him in Turkey, and he knew not where to turn after the war. All his money had gone: he received no pay from his Government, for there was no Government. He had had no news of his relations since the revolution swallowed them up, and he said he knew no way of earning his living except on a ship of war; yet he was cheerful in a rather plaintive way. Poor Commander Burikoff! I hope he has found some haven of refuge.

On the whole, the Russians, as I must continue to call them, kept very much to themselves, though there were exceptions to this general rule. They spoke many tongues, but few of them knew any English, and not very many of them French. Uncle Vodka used to talk to us in pigeon-Turkish, and a few of the British knew a little Russian, notably two young Australians. Australians beat all varieties of British in their search for knowledge. The Russians were bitterly poor. They had no Embassy money, for they had no protecting Embassy. How they managed to live at all was very wonderful. The sailors had started with full kits, unlike prisoners of war, who were taken in what they have on; but they had gradually sold their clothes for food until they had not much left. The Turks did not actually let them starve, but they went very near it, and in the winter they nearly froze. We helped them sometimes, but they were too proud to be helped much, and we had not much to give, there were so many of them. In the summer of 1918 they used to go in gangs to the river, armed with every conceivable kind of drag-net, and sweep that river clean. Fish they caught in large quantities and ate them; it was about the only meat they got: and they caught crayfish, which they sold to the British. They did not emulate some of the British, who caught frogs and ate them, so far as I know. Perhaps there was no sustenance in frogs. I ate one one day, but he must have been the wrong kind. It was said that they ate cats and I'm sure I hope they did. The French used to eat the tortoises that scour the plains of Anatolia.

My best friend among the Russians was a colonel, a Georgian prince. He got me to teach him English, and he would write down the equivalent of a word in Russian, French, German, Polish, or Georgian quite indiscriminately. He was a fine, brave little fellow; dark, muscular, and astonishingly fiery. I expect he is with Denikin's army now, fighting Bolsheviki. "Ces sales types," as he used to call them. Years ago, during some minor outbreak in Russia, his squadron had arrested Lenin and brought him in, and the colonel spent vain hours in wishing he had slain him then and there. Europe would probably echo his lament.

If Maslûm escapes the gallows, woe betide him if ever he meets the Russian colonel. He will be killed inevitably. After the frightful punishment of Constantine B. the colonel protested vigorously, and got the poor fellow put into hospital. Not very long afterwards, a sort of commission of Turkish officials, accompanied, I believe, by a member of the Spanish Embassy, visited Afion to look into the question of the Russian prisoners' treatment. Maslûm Bey did not wish his conduct to be exposed, so he visited the colonel and had the effrontery to offer him a bribe of an oke (2¼ lb.) of sugar to say nothing about it. The little man was furious, and swore that if ever he met that man with arms in his hand he would kill him on sight. I sincerely trust he will be robbed by the British of any such opportunity. When the commission came he spoke up at once, but nothing came of it except that the colonel was locked up for about a week. He had a little house to himself up a side street, and I often used to visit him there and devise ways of persuading him to accept little presents of tea or other things from parcels; for he never got parcels, and was miserably poor. It was really quite a dangerous thing to do, and I had never to let anyone else see. He was about as safe to handle as a live bomb with the pin out. The head of the commission referred to above accused him of secretly handing a document to the Spaniard. The Colonel had not done so, and he said so, expecting his word to be accepted. But the fool of a Turk, who had probably never met an honest man in his life, expressed himself still unsatisfied. Up flared the colonel. "Search the man!" he said. "If you find it on him I will commit suicide. If not, you shall." The Turk apologized.

There was a Russo-Armenian, a sneak-thief, and he robbed an Indian officer of some tobacco. The Indian suspected him and laid a trap into which he fell. I saw the Russian colonel tell him off in the street, while the man trembled and went pale green, and afterwards the Colonel told me what he said.

"Have you a revolver?" he asked. "No, sir."

"Have you a good razor?" "No, sir."

"Then borrow a rope and hang yourself. You have brought shame on the Russian officers. If you are alive at the end of the war, I shall send you a pistol. Use it. If you fail, I shall send a man to kill you, for you are too base for me to fight."

He was a dangerous little man, but he had many friends among the English, and his ambition was to ride in the Grand National. May he win through!

He had been in the Imperial Guard, and knew all the Petrograd Court gossip. One day, during the English lesson, he saw the announcement of the death of a certain Grand Duke in the paper, and told me a tale about him. The Grand Duke was a parallel, in position only, to the Duke of Connaught, for he was an uncle of the Tsar, and he was Governor of Turkestan. At the Tsar's coronation, it was his privilege to hold the crown during part of the ceremony, and, while doing so, he became enamoured of a vast ruby which it contained—call it the Kohinur to complete the parallel. The stone glistened, and he desired it very greatly, so he bit it from its setting and hid it in his cheek. But he was observed, and brought to book. He was required to take up his residence in Siberia; and here the story ought to end, "and he lived happily for long afterwards." Perhaps he did, for the colonel told me that, being already married, in Siberia he committed bigamy, to annoy his nephew.

Russians are very direct people. When they desire a thing they straightway pursue it. There was a very large Russian officer in Afion who went by the name of Uncle Vodka. He was an old man, a dug-out, and he fought at the siege of Plevna in 1877-79. He was about 6 ft. 5 in. high, and very huge. He had a long, broad beard, and looked like a picture of the Tsar's coachman. He was a direct person. He conceived the ambition of colouring his body, as a man might colour a meerschaum pipe, and he chose the hill-side to do it on. There he would lie in the sun without a single stitch of clothing on his great body, which must have been nearly a rood in area, and he would turn himself round and round so as to make the colour even all over. We used to climb the hill on purpose to see him, and he was always pleased to meet us. He was a venerable figure. You might have taken him for an archdeacon.

Among all these Russians, differing as they did in caste and kind, there was one thing they held in common. Despite the mother revolution and all its children, they still held their belief in Russia, great and united. Technically speaking, many of them were the subjects of countries now at war with each other and with us. But, although the conditions they lived in were far worse than ours in the matter of overcrowding, they clove together as Russians. I studied this question, and used to get one to interpret for others, so that my survey might be based broadly; and in that one respect I found them all the same. There are no boundaries, they would say, between Russia and Ukrainia, or between Russia and the Cossacks. Poland they excepted, and, to some extent, Georgia; but they denied that the new divisions of the rest of Russia could endure. There was neither racial, physical, nor lingual frontier they maintained. And when I asked whether they did not find it difficult to avoid thorny subjects, now that their country was giving birth to republics almost daily, and was torn in pieces by internal war, they said No; they had all been taken prisoner as allies of each other and of us, and allies they still were. The only exceptions, among the officers, were a hybrid anarchist who joined the Turks, and the Russo-Armenian sneak-thief.

Russians all call each other by their Christian names. I once asked a Russian midshipman what he called the captain of his ship. "George," he replied. "And what on the quarter-deck?" I asked. "George, son of Dmitri," he said. I should like to be present to hear Admiral Beatty called David by a midshipman on the quarter-deck of the "Queen Elizabeth."

CHAPTER XIII

THE BERNE CONVENTION

AFTER hanging fire for a very long time, the Berne Convention between Great Britain and the Sublime Porte was signed, and in the course of time copies reached Afion-Kara-Hissar.

It seemed to us to be framed so that a coach-and-four could be driven through every one of its clauses. But, we were winning the war, and a great many of its provisions were applied. It was our Magna Charta.

Under this convention a large number of prisoners were to be exchanged at once, 300 British and 700 Indians against 1,500 Turks, as far as I can remember.

Of course we all wanted to be included. We had not known how mad we were to be included until that ray of hope appeared. It seemed as though we suddenly saw ourselves as we were, as new prisoners saw us when they arrived, men grown listless and almost hopeless, with brave words on their lips and chill in their hearts. Of the 300 British we could not all hope to be, but for the others there was a further hope, for, according to the Convention, periodical medical boards were to be held, and all those suffering from any of a given list of disabilities were to be exchanged too.

There was a great deal of heart-burning, and the camp was the prey of winged rumours, most of them discouraging ones. I can scarcely bear to think of that time even now.

The Kut prisoners thought that their five months' siege ought to be included in the period of their captivity. It was only natural that they should. But even so, we old-timers had been far longer confined than they had. Then there was the question of age, and the older of us did boast of our years, and wish inwardly that we had added to their number when first registered by the Turks. Were married men to have, other things being equal, any consideration? That was another question, and men added to the number of their children, if not of their wives.

These are but a few of the questions that troubled us.

But, in the end, the Turks ignored much of the Convention, and began to hold medical boards to sort out those who were incapacitated for further fighting.

On the 8th of August, 1918, the first board sat in Afion. There were two Turkish doctors on it, and one British, Capt. Startin, R.A.M.C. But as one of the Turks made his own decisions, and the other merely said "peki," which means "I concur," and as the decision went by a majority of votes, the British member did not have much chance. Still, he did succeed in steering most of the really deserving cases through, and he did his very best for all of us, seizing every slightest opportunity and displaying both diplomatic skill and doggedness to a high degree.

Of course everyone wanted to be tested. "You can't win a lottery unless you take a ticket," as someone put it. And when the day came, and the board assembled in a room at the Medrisseh, there was far more of us than could be got through in a day. We sat in the shade of the poplar trees, in front of the mosque, and when each officer who had been examined came out he was bombarded with questions, and surrounded by an anxious crowd. But no decisions were announced, and the British representative was sworn to secrecy, which oath he kept. How he managed to I am sure I don't know, for the excitement was intense. British excitement, hardly admitted at all, but gnawing at the vitals, like the Spartan boy's fox. So no one knew whether he had been passed or not, though all were agreed that the senior Turkish doctor was an unpleasant creature, jocular and offensive, and very hard to satisfy. The fact was that he knew little or nothing of his job, found difficulty in understanding the terms of reference, hated the British, and distrusted everyone in the world.

That day passed in hidden agony.

The next day, the third anniversary of my capture, my turn came. I did not think there was much chance, but had faint hopes that some hidden doom might reveal itself to the trained skill of a doctor. Really the only things wrong with me were that I had lost three and a half stone in weight and had lumbago. So when asked to strip and to state what my claim was based on I said lumbago. The senior Turkish doctor never glanced at my lumbago region at all. But he laid me down and performed some of the mysteries of his craft. And all the time he kept on talking to me. We had quite an argument in French. He asked me why I knew no Turkish, and I replied that it was too dangerous, that Maslûm Bey had sent officers to gaol for knowing Turkish; and this was perfectly true, though it was not my reason. I did not want to lumber my brain with Turkish. Also, as a writer of codes, and in order to avoid suspicion generally, it had never been my object to display much intelligence to Turks. It was too dangerous, as I said. Not that I pretended to be mad, as did two officers of another camp who were successful in bamboozling the best Turkish doctors, on the contrary I pretended to be sane. I did not "wangle," to use the term in vogue, one particle. The doctor further cross-examined me. Whey did I wish to leave Turkey? he asked. I said I wanted to see my wife and daughter. We came to a little bickering, and, in spite of my deficient French, repartee came to me quicker than to him, and I won.

The verdict did not come until some days later. Several of the most necessitous cases had been rejected; for instance, an officer with a double hernia and an officer suffering from genuine fits. One man who had lost an eye was included, another rejected. And several perfectly able-bodied officers and men had been included.

I was included myself. But not for lumbago. I was passed unfit on the score of being mad.

 The senior Turkish doctor failed to understand my simple nature, and turning to his colleague, he said, "I think he is mad." The colleague duly responded "Peki"; the British officer, who understood Turkish and acted as interpreter told Startin, and that best of men said I had been very queer for some time back. He was perfectly right. We were all as queer as queer could be. The good fellow took the first chance of reassuring me, but it was no good. I used to get people on whom I could rely, privately in corners (bystanders were buttonholed and prayed with, as the *War Cry* used to print), and ask them as man to man whether I was really mad. They all said no. But it was no good. I thought that, even if not mad, I must at least have very shaken nerves, and continued to think so until, months after, at Alexandria, a kind-hearted pilot took me up in an aeroplane, and stunted me scientifically, loops and double loops, spinning nose dives, and side slips, and other glories of the air. Never having been within half a mile of an aeroplane before, this convinced me that my nerves were still fairly sound; for I came down half drunken with the splendour of it all, ate a hearty meal, and went through it all again the same afternoon. It was like drinking champagne on top of a mountain; and for the first time since being a prisoner I was glad not to have lived a century earlier.

But once I was a certified lunatic, and have never been uncertified since.

After the medical board came a few dreadful weeks. Every day brought forth a new rumour. We heard that the Germans had refused safe-conduct to the repatriation ship, and it was true. We heard that the medical board at Broussa, which had passed some of the generals there, had been squashed, and that a new board had rejected them; and it was true. We heard that the sickest men of all, who had been sent to Constantinople for exchange some time back—an old R.C. padre with a bad heart, a youngster with nearly every disability a man may have and live, and others—had been rejected. And that was true, too, for they came back to us again.

It was a perfectly awful time, and won't bear writing about.

At last, on the 9th of September, we received orders to leave for Smyrna by the evening train.

There had been a perfect epidemic of escape projects recently. It was partly caused by sheer weariness of spirit, partly by a leading mind recently installed among us, partly by encouragement through secret messages from England, and partly by a hope of joining the exchange train and mixing unnoticed with the lucky ones. There were several sorts of would-be escapers. The best sort thought things out thoroughly, kept their mouths shut, and went. The worst sort talked about it frequently, for years, and did not go. The first were greatly to be admired; but the second were a pest to the whole camp in a land where the whole community suffered for the escapade of one. All the escapers who actually started were brave men, and I wish more of them had got through.

The day we started for Smyrna, for we did start, a party of three escaped; and the escape was not discovered by the Turks until we were in the train. There were thirteen officers, and I forget how many men, and we were counted and recounted several times. Then all the luggage vans were searched through and all the large boxes opened, and the train was searched from end to end. But the three were not found, they were far away in the hills. So we left Afion under suspicion, and with armed guards in every carriage to prevent anyone from boarding the train.

Our last view of the camp was most affecting. There was a spontaneous outburst of noble good feeling and unselfish gladness, unmixed with any envy of our good luck. None of us thought the end of the war was near, yet those who stayed behind cheered those who went, with never a sign of an afterthought. It was not just a few, it was everyone; and we literally had to struggle through the crowd in the street with our arms aching from hearty handshakes. It is a very splendid last memory of Afion.

I had been there two years and seven months.

CHAPTER XIV

SMYRNA

OUR first night in the train was rather uncomfortably crowded, but we would not have minded being piled in heaps on that journey. In the morning we reached a place called Ushak, and there had rather a shock, for all thirteen officers were ushered into a dirty shed and informed that it was a hospital, and that we were all to be examined for cholera. This was more serious than appears on the face of it, for two of our party were rather out of sorts, and a Turkish doctor would be quite liable to mistake this malady for cholera. Then good-bye to hope for them. They would have been put in some disgusting place with all manner of afflicted people, and it is by no means improbable that they would have died. The Turkish doctor had an assistant with a microscope, but we didn't trust either of them one bit: so we refused to be examined. I can't enter into details, but we refused unanimously to do what they required. There was an impasse. We could not proceed without health certificates, for there were quarantine regulations in force. Of course, we could, in the last resource, bribe the doctor, but we preferred not to. We stood fast upon the dignity of British officers, and said they did not do that kind of thing. It was much cheaper to bluff than to bribe, and we wanted all our money. I suggested to the Turkish officer in charge that he should hire a peasant to be examined on our behalf, and offered to pay the man ten piastres for his courtesy. But that obviously sound suggestion was ruled out as being unscientific. The honour of the medical profession and the prestige of the microscope had to be upheld. It ended in a compromise. The doctor agreed to accept three delegates as representatives of the whole party. Three strong men volunteered to be examined, and we threatened them with all manner of revenge if they proved to have any obscure disease that would hold us up. But they passed the ordeal safely and we were solemnly granted thirteen clean bills of health and allowed to proceed.

The men were detained for examination, despite all we could do, but they reached Smyrna a day later without mishap. As it turned out, they were lucky to be late.

The approach to Smyrna from inland is a very beautiful journey. The railway runs through the fruitful valley of Magnina, flanked by great hills, and full of vineyards and groves of figs and olives.

We were travelling in comfort now. Our second night had been passed in a truck, rather hilariously, I am afraid, for three of us celebrated an Old

Wykehamist dinner and sang "Domum" most of the night through. For the last few hours of the journey we had the company of a Roman Catholic priest, a quiet, gentle, young man from Austria, very sad about the condition of his country and very much concerned at all the excesses of the Turks. He found his hard life a very hopeless struggle against corruption and cruelty of every kind. I had not up to then met so thoroughly pro-British an enemy.

We reached the Point station at Smyrna early in the afternoon. Where we were to be lodged we did not know. The Turkish officer in charge of us had treated us well; he was the only member of the staff of Maslûm Bey who had come through the inquiry without a single charge against him. But he had no influence, and he was very junior; moreover, he laboured under unjust suspicion of having assisted the three officers who escaped the day we left Afion. We heard their fate later on, and it may as well be recorded here. They had only got two or three days' journey into the hills when they were captured by brigands, who debated for some time what to do with them. At last one of them thought he saw a chance of escape, and made a dash; but he was shot, and the others two were released and driven away. They were not allowed to assist their companion, and he was last seen wounded and in the hands of the brigands. His two companions gave themselves up to the nearest Turkish authorities and succeeded in getting a search party sent out. They tried hard to be allowed, on temporary parole, to accompany the party, but were refused permission and their friend has not been heard of since. Earlier in the war, after the fall of Antwerp, he had been interned in Holland, but had escaped, and eventually joined the R.N.A.S. It was indeed hard luck that he should die in an unsuccessful second escape only seven weeks before Turkey went out of the war.

Guided by the Turkish officer, we walked through the streets of Smyrna to the military headquarters, a large building that faced a public garden, where the band played in the afternoons and children disported themselves with their nurses.

Our reception was very chilly. Our friendly officer was a very small person here, and could do nothing for us; and we could not find anyone who knew anything about us. They had never heard of any Berne Convention or of any arrangement for exchange of prisoners, and they suspected us all of having escaped and been sent there for punishment. For a long time we waited in a passage, wondering what would be the upshot of it all, and then the usual thing happened, for we were cast into gaol. After all our visions of a week or two of absolute liberty while waiting for the ship, this was a terrible anti-climax. We were thrust into the military lock-up, and two sentries with fixed bayonets were placed at the door.

It was a dark and very dirty room, with a broken wooden floor that long experience warned us against lying on, and there were no chairs or furniture of any kind. Five Indian officers were thrown into it with us, and were as indignant as we. There was no one to appeal to. Our senior officer, the only one who spoke Turkish, had remained at the station to watch our baggage, and the officer who had escorted us had gone back to him. After a while an interpreter came to us, and we urged him to fetch a senior officer who could hear our complaint. A long time after this a very hard-faced and thoroughly Prussianised Turkish colonel came in with the interpreter, and we explained that we were sick men sent down for exchange. He listened coldly, and said he knew nothing about that, and that we were very well where we were. Afterwards the interpreter told us he was in a bad temper because seven hundred of his regiment had deserted to the hills, and he had only discovered it that morning.

We looked out through the bars rather dolefully, and watched the rank and fashion of Smyrna in the garden. There seemed little hope of getting out, or of getting any food in, and our bedding was at the station.

Again a typically Turkish thing occurred. There was a privy just outside the door, the other side of the sentries. One officer was compelled to ask permission to go to it. The request was passed out by the sentries, and the officer was led out into the garden, before all the women and children. This was the more unnecessary because the proper place was there, just across the passage. It may be that Turks do not consider this sort of exhibition objectionable, but to an Englishman or to an Indian officer it is more humiliating than any private cruelty. It was a studied policy of the Turks to play upon our sensitiveness to indecency. The unspeakable Turk: with all our languages and vocabularies we never found a phrase to rival that: unspeakable he was and unspeakable he is.

Suddenly the "strafe" ended. The British chaplain had got to know of our plight, and had gained the ear of someone in authority. After having paced the streets of Smyrna as comparatively free men on the way from the station, we were taken in close marching order between guards with fixed bayonets to a very dirty Turkish officers' hotel and given rooms. A sentry with a fixed bayonet sat on a chair at the end of the passage. We of the Old Wykehamist dinner shared a room, and I slept like a top: the others tossed and moaned, and in the morning slew a vast number of intruders, many hundreds. But this hotel was our very last experience of these pests, for life, I hope.

The next day the Vali came to see us, Rahmy Bey, the governor of the province of Aidin. After his visit all the frowns turned to smiles, for he was known to favour good treatment of the subjects of the Entente.

A day or two later we moved once more, this time in the greatest comfort. Can you but gain one gesture of protection from a great man in an Eastern country, you may go in peace, for the underlings are but looking-glasses to reflect his mood.

 We drove in carriages to the station, and travelled first class a few miles by rail to the suburb called Paradise. That is its name since Roman times, and it was Paradise indeed to us.

We were established in the fine buildings of the International College, an American foundation with a Canadian in charge of it as principal. Dr. Maclachlan was his name, and he and Mr. Reed, an American gentleman who is second in command, gave us the warmest, kindest welcome in the world. They and the ladies of the staff had a sumptuous tea awaiting us, and everything that man or woman could do they did. We had not known the like for many years.

There is a little colony of British and Americans at Paradise, and everyone of them deserves to be there. The whole great building was at our disposal: dormitories for the men, small rooms for the officers, a school conduit to wash in, shower baths, electric light, a fine library, and perfect cleanliness. It was the cleanliness of the building and the kindness of their hearts that appealed to us. I confess without any shame that it almost broke me down. And there were children to play with, bright, merry, little American and English children. As our men came in, some on crutches, some limping, all of them thin and weary, I saw one of those kind hosts of ours pick up a crippled Indian sepoy on his back and carry him up the stairs. They nursed our sick, they mended and washed our clothes, they cooked dainty little dishes for the convalescents, and they gave us all heart once more. We were unclean and uncivilized, queerer perhaps than we knew, and they brought back to us the knowledge that the world as a whole is good.

It must not be imagined that all our troubles were over. We were still in Turkey. The officer who had charge of us was a Cretan Turk, a kind-hearted but rather diffident man. He received his orders from one army corps, and the officer in charge of the guard from another. The result was chaos: for while the Cretan gave us very considerable privileges, his plans were defeated by the officer of the guard, a conceited little puppy of about nineteen, who did nothing but swagger about with a sword. He was wholly malicious and possibly a little bit wrong in the head. He tormented the good lady who nursed our worst cases by telling her the bloody deeds he itched to do; the finest sensation on earth, he said, was to feel your steel pass through an enemy's body. But she turned upon him and told him that in a few months he would be selling melons on the street for a living. When the Cretan, who was a senior captain, gave us leave to go out into the ample grounds of the college, this little squirt ordered the guard to prevent us; and in like way he made himself so intolerable that Dr. Maclachlan spoke to a higher power and got him removed. After that things went quite smoothly.

There was a very large playing field attached to the college, twenty acres, I think it was; there was a chapel with an organ in it, an auditorium with a grand piano, and a large, well-equipped gymnasium. We began by using a few rooms of the main building, and ended by filling the whole establishment, even the chapel. For parties were coming in almost daily from all over Turkey. At first they were nearly all sick men, some of them at the very point of death. We lost sixteen men in Smyrna, who died before they could be exchanged, almost within sight of home. But later on, when the Turks found they could not make up the thousand in any other way, all the camps were combed through again, and a great many of the later arrivals had nothing whatever the matter with them except the awful disease of prison weariness: a disease that, fortunately, few people know, but which none who have known it will ever forget.

It was astonishing at first to realize how few really sick men there were, but the explanation was not far to seek: the sick had died. Some of those who passed medical boards were almost ludicrous. One, I remember, had an abnormally rough and thick skin, had had it all his life. Another had complained that he felt tired. Another had been late for the medical board, in fact, he had only gone up for a joke, and at the last moment; but he pleaded that he had rested so many times by the way that he could not get there in time. He was one of the best football players in Turkey, but he was passed.

Another large contingent came from Afion, others from Broussa, Constantinople, Gedos—the parole camp, where officers who chose to give their parole could go and enjoy almost complete liberty; from Angora, and from all the camps in the Taurus mountains. These last were the weakest of the whole. They were the survivors of a terrible slavery.

The European community of Smyrna, save for about a week near the beginning of the war, had been allowed to live in their own houses and to go where they pleased in Smyrna and its widespread suburbs. They will perhaps disagree with me when I say that they had been very well treated. This was due to the political sagacity of the Vali, Rahmy Bey, who seems to have realized from the beginning that Turkey was on the wrong side. He has been accused of vast speculations, and he certainly tolerated massacre and wholesale deportation of the Greeks; but he protected the Armenians in his province, and spread his cloak over the subjects of the Entente. For that we must be very grateful. I met him several times and found him clever, strong, and amusing. He is a very notable Turk, and may rule Turkey some day.

Many of the French and British subjects came to visit us, and, later, when we were free, we enjoyed much hospitality at their hands. One of them told me that the dearth of news was so great during the beginning of the German retreat that smuggled copies of the *Times* newspaper had commanded the enormous price of one pound per hour of perusal.

We waited on and on. The college was filled to overflowing, and another camp was started in another part of Smyrna. Nobody knew when the ship would come, or even where it would come to. But the resistance of the enemy was crumbling. Turkish officers told us that their armies were mere skeleton forces. They estimated that there were six hundred thousand deserters in the hills. A story was told of a battalion ordered from Smyrna to the Palestine front, which melted on the railway journey until there was only one man left besides the C.O. Bulgaria gave way. The Palestine front gave way, and a Turkish staff officer told me that their estimate of losses there alone was ninety-two thousand men. It was plain that the war was coming to an end.

Exactly two weeks before Turkey actually signed the Armistice we were set free, absolutely free. Some officers were received into the houses of residents in Bournabat, the chief suburb of Smyrna; some went into hotels where meals cost whole fortunes; some stayed on in the College; and, with three others, I rented a small furnished house just outside the College gates. It belonged to a Mrs. Constantine, the wife of a Greek gentleman, a master at the College. He was a man who had travelled, and lived in America, and he was heartily on our side. But the conscription had netted him in as a transport driver, and he was believed to be now a prisoner in British hands. We tried to console poor Mrs. Constantine by telling her that he would be quite safe there, much safer than with the Turks; but she wanted him back, poor soul, and so did little Chloe and Aeneas, his children.

During this fortnight we did as we pleased, and enjoyed life.

More than one family among the European residents were exceedingly kind to us, and made us free of their homes.

It was also my good fortune, through Mrs. Reed, to make the acquaintance of some Greek ladies, and more whole-hearted fiery patriots I have never listened to. The Peace Conference is now, as I write, ponderously considering the future of Turkey, and their fate still hangs in the balance. The Smyrna Greeks long for union with Greece, long for it as a sailor longs for the sea, although they know that it may bring them poverty; for the district of Smyrna is rich in comparison with Greek proper, and would perhaps be bled to feed Athens. They know that, but they burn to throw off the tyranny of the Turks. Who can but sympathize with them?

The European permanent residents, on the other hand, wish for the Turks to remain, for by accommodating the chief Turkish officials they can make much money. But they are in a vast minority to the Greeks; they are aliens, and the Greeks were there two thousand years before the Turks were. They should have no say in the matter, beyond what is just. Their say in this matter should be governed by the extent to which they aided the war, on the Entente side. This I may say without a breach of hospitality, for of the only two houses I went into, one real English and the other French, there was not one member who was eligible for fighting; and the people of Paradise did contribute their sons to the war, but they are not permanent residents. Under the capitulations a very strange community grew up in Turkey. All sorts of people assumed British, French, or Italian nationality for the sake of the protection it gave them. They speak all tongues, more or less, and the "British" among them are often less like Englishmen than are the Eurasians of India. There are many families of "British" who can speak no English at all; nearly all the rest, except the rare ones who have been educated "at home," speak what, further East, we call Chichi English. They are "British" in inverted commas, and they "supported" our cause mostly in inverted commas too.

Whether the Turks' own claim to Smyrna is a just one I am not competent to judge. The mere fact that they have hideously misgoverned should not invalidate their claim provided that they are in a genuine majority, not a majority obtained by deportation and massacre. For their system of Government can be improved and kept watch over.

What is to be the future of the Turks, in any case?

That they should hold no subject countries is obvious. But in their own country, where they do actually form the majority of the population, what is their future? Their official classes are abominable people. They can oppress, but they have no aptitude for the wider forms of business and banking, building and organizing, or any form of creative work. A Turkish financier is more Hooligan than Hooley. They cannot compete with the Christians in bloodless ventures. We used to dream of various fates for them, but the fate that is coming is worse than we dreamed. They are bankrupt; there will soon be neither pay nor pension for most of them. While they still ruled Armenia, Mesopotamia, Syria, Palestine, and the coasts of Arabia, their system was simple. The "educated" Turk got a post in some branch of the Government service, with small pay, but a large income. The pay came from the Government, and the income from the subject peoples. But that time is gone, and, as the Turkish officer was told, they will soon be selling melons on the streets. Metaphorically that is what they will be doing. They will be driven to trade; and wherever a Turk sits down to trade an Armenian will sit and he will beggar that Turk. They are waiting to do it, and looking forward to it.

The Turks tried to govern by an absolute king, and it failed. They tried to govern by a *soi disant* representative assembly, and that failed; it degenerated into a tyranny by a small clique, and that tyranny failed too. An oligarchy is out of the question, for there are no families in Turkey from which it could be recruited. There remain soviets, but the Turkish peasant is not nearly advanced enough for that. It is even doubtful if any race on earth is. The Turkish peasant is to the full as backward as, or more backward than, the Indian peasant, and he has much fewer brains. It seems to be more a question of evolution than of revolution for the Turks. From our little way up the cliff of civilisation we look down to the Turk, and he seems too far away for us to lend him a helping hand.

The Turkish people do not include a middle class or an aristocracy. The reasons will be found in any good history of their slave theory of government, but the reasons concern Europe less than does the fact. With a small margin of error, all Turks may be described as falling in one of two categories, namely, officials and peasants. My opinion of the officials must be plain to anyone who has read thus far, and needs no reinforcing. But the peasants have a great many very good qualities. They are brave, cheerful, and very patient people, hospitable and generous by nature, and the simplest of the simple. They lie and steal much less than do the Christians in their land, and infinitely less than their own officials. On the other hand, they are stupid, and they have been for centuries so inured to brutality that they value human life and human pain not at all. If you strayed into a Turkish village you would probably be treated as a guest, and given of their best. But you might see these same villagers sally forth to burn, rape, and kill in a neighbouring village of Christians.

The only future for Turkey seems to be for the whole race to go back to the land until from the soil there rises a middle class able in the course of time to produce rulers of men. In the meantime, some European Power or America should have a mandate, not only the League of Nations' mandate, but the Turks' own mandate, to do for them the things they cannot do; to provide judges and governors, railway and postal controllers, and to officer a police force. Personally, I believe they would, by British or Americans, be the easiest people on earth to rule.

I must write one word on our other enemies, the Germans in Turkey. There was a German in the Taurus who boasted that, by his treatment of British prisoners, he had killed more enemies than anyone on the Western front. But he was almost alone in that respect. With few exceptions, Germans in Turkey treated Britishers in misfortune as brother white men in an Eastern land. Especially was this so in the air service, where chivalry ran higher than in any other branch of the fighting. German airmen who had brought a Britisher down always treated him well; very often they went over our lines and, at the risk of their machines or their lives, dropped a note from the captured one asking that his kit might be sent along. Then one of our machines would fly back, unmolested, and drop the kit. There were several officers in Afion who had received their kit in this way. There was also an officer who had been defeated in a fight in the air, and to whom his victor gave his own silver watch with an inscription engraved upon it commemorating the combat. The German passed through Afion long afterwards, and came to see if he could do anything more to help his late enemy. Another officer in Afion was taken prisoner in Palestine, in thin clothes, and had to proceed up to Afion, where it was cold. In the train he met a German officer who was going on leave home, and this man divided up his shirts, his socks, and his underclothes, and fitted the Englishman out. Since coming to England I have seen in the papers that a clergyman was fined £10 for giving a German prisoner some tobacco, and a farmer 40s. for giving a German prisoner half a loaf and a bottle of ginger-beer. Is there not a better way of looking at things than this? I am not pro-German, very far from it, but I am pro anything generous or kind, and I know what it is to be a prisoner.

CHAPTER XV

THE SHIP

AT last the ship came, and lay off Phokea, outside the Gulf of Smyrna.

We went off in tugs, out of that lovely bay, more beautiful, to my mind, than the bay of Naples, and we went on board the Australian hospital ship "Kanowna," where they gave us a royal welcome.

This was the 1st of November, 1918.

August the 9th, 1915—*November the 1st*, 1918.

They had many cots prepared, expecting many sick and cripples. They asked as we came on board where the sick were, and we replied that they were dead.

Phokea was a beautiful little Greek town when war broke out; it has vineyards and olive groves behind it, and it looks out on the bluest of bays. It had once been inhabited by Greek subjects of the Turks, but now it lay bare and empty, with hollow windows staring at the sea. There was an old Englishman on board, a civilian who had been many years in Smyrna, and him I asked why it lay thus desolate. "When the Turks declared a Jihad," he said, "a holy war, soldiers and a rabble came to Phokea, and crucified the Greek men upon olive trees; the women they raped and then cut their hands and feet off. What happened to the children I do not know."

There our last sun set on Turkey, and we steamed away to the South.

FOOTNOTES:

[1] The complete figures, according to information received up to 25th October:—

BRITISH PRISONERS OF WAR IN TURKEY.

	Believed captured.	Repatriated, Escaped, or Released.	Died.	Untraced.	Still prisoners
Officers—					
British	472	43	14	None	415
Indian	231	7	7	None	21

Total officers	703	50	21	None	632
Other ranks—					
British	4,932	279	1,840	449	2,364
Indian	10,948	1,177	1,429	1,773	6,569
Total other ranks	15,880	1,456	3,269	2,222	8,933
Total all ranks	16,583	1,506	3,290	2,222	9,565

[2] A fellow prisoner, who was kind enough to read through the MS. of this book for me, contributes the following note:—

"To do our difficulties justice I think you ought to say that besides the loss of value of paper against gold, the rise of prices reduced the purchasing power of the £Tq to *one-twentieth* of what it was in the summer of 1915. This is strictly true. I have a list of the prices of ordinary commodities up to Spring, 1918. Actually the purchasing value of £20 from England was between twenty and twenty-four shillings in the winter 1917-18 as compared to the early Autumn, 1915."—A.D.P.